Periodical Press and Colonial Modernity

Periodical Press
and
Colonial Modernity

Odisha, 1866–1936

Sachidananda Mohanty

OXFORD
UNIVERSITY PRESS

OXFORD
UNIVERSITY PRESS

Oxford University Press is a department of the University of Oxford.
It furthers the University's objective of excellence in research, scholarship,
and education by publishing worldwide. Oxford is a registered trademark of
Oxford University Press in the UK and in certain other countries

Published in India by
Oxford University Press
YMCA Library Building, 1 Jai Singh Road, New Delhi 110 001, India

ISBN-13: 978-0-19-946147-9
ISBN-10: 0-19-946147-3

Typeset in Adobe Jenson Pro 11/14
by The Graphics Solution, New Delhi 110 092
Printed and bound in India at Repro India Ltd., Mumbai

For

my late parents,

Bidyut Prabha Devi and Panchanan Mohanty

and

Ma (Banaj Patnaik)

Contents

Preface

No one remotely connected with the study of cultural history can pass over the significance of periodical press/literature. Its instrumental value for understanding history, society, culture, politics, indeed the very texture of our daily life, has been recognized for long.

And yet, periodical press, as a genre, remains an area of darkness, a relic of the past for students of English and comparative literature, while historians of many persuasions have rightly appropriated the genre for their own ends.

Periodical press/literature is not a dated concept and category, it has a living presence. It is a fascinating field whose contours are still unknown to most: The editorial style, patterns of circulation and patronage systems, funding and readership, institutional support and resistance, censorship and court cases of the periodical press still elude us in great many areas.

Periodical literature casts its looming shadow on the present. Its presence is felt in the Internet and digital media, in the research arena in contemporary academic discourse, and systems of knowledge. Its manner of bringing together the best thought in a given field and showing the evolution of thinking on a subject of study remain perennially relevant to all academic and scholarly endeavours.

This book brings back our attention to the periodical press by relating it to colonial modernity in Odisha during the late nineteenth and early twentieth centuries. According to historian Dilip Menon (2002: 1662):

The term modernity comes to us masking both its origins within a distinct geographical space as well as an imagination almost entirely concerned with a description of change in Europe and America (what we refer to euphemistically as the West). It is precisely because the term modernity appears to be neither temporally [n]or geographically grounded that there is an increasing suspicion towards its relevance as a term for understanding historical change.

My aim here is to locate colonial modernity and its alternative in a specific geographical and temporal space, the only way it could gain significance.

How did the modernity project emerge and evolve in Odisha during the Raj? What were its contours? What were the commonalities and differences between the colonial modernity in Odisha and Bengal and its European counterpart, based on the Enlightenment 'virtues' of 'Rationality, Universality and Progress' (Breckenridge et al. 2002: 6)? Was this modernity entirely consensual, or was it contested in the pages of the periodicals through what has come to be known as alternative or vernacular modernity? This study attempts to show how periodical press shaped ideas and the material culture of a region, and in turn got metamorphosed by the play of contemporary cultural and ideological forces. In other words, it would be interesting to study the contestatory discourse surrounding colonial and vernacular modernity.

While the study deals with the role of periodical press/literature as a whole in the context of Odisha's colonial past, it concentrates on two periodicals, *Utkal Dipika* and *Utkal Sahitya*, along with their founder-editors, Gourishankar Ray and Biswanath Kar, for better effect.

It has been a fascinating experience for me over the years, to go through the journals in Odisha that operated during the late nineteenth and early twentieth centuries. Handling the moth-eaten copies or their digital versions has its own charm and challenges. Unravelling the vast complexity of cultures, histories, traditions, and lifestyles is truly a staggering task, at times overwhelming. The selection of items remains a primary challenge. Along with this, there is the need to offer a coherent account in the face of what Shyam Benegal calls the 'unreliable cultural memory'.

The study of periodical press and colonial modernity in Odisha shows the way people asked questions regarding the challenges they faced in the past. We can learn from their experience and perhaps ask better questions regarding the many issues that continue to plague us today. The questions of taxation, governance, censorship, and participatory democracy, peculiar to colonial modernity, are as alive today as then. Literary issues like editing, canon-making, translation, adaptation and plagiarism are relevant now as they were then. Hopefully, this study will appeal to a multidisciplinary audience and lay readers as well, and underline the centrality of the periodical press in the discourse of colonial modernity.

A Note Regarding the Use of Terms in This Book

The region being discussed in this book has been conventionally known as Orissa, and its people Oriyas. Utkal and Kalinga are also terms used to denote the same region, though they actually refer to different political formations in historical times, related to the people of this region.

In response to a long-standing demand of the people of the region, the government of India, by a gazette notification a few years ago, changed the name Orissa to Odisha, and consequently the people of the region are known today as Odias.

In this book, the terms Odia and Odisha are generally used; I have retained Oriya and Orissa at some places to be true to the expressions earlier used in texts and documents.

Acknowledgements

I would like to thank the following individuals and institutions, among others, for their help: the Odisha State Archives and the Odisha State Library (Bhubaneswar); private collections of late Brajanath Rath at Balasore; Nikhil Patnaik, Pushpashree Patnaik, and Srujanika (an organization based in Bhubaneswar); Indira Gandhi Memorial Library (Hyderabad) and National Library (Kolkata); students, faculty, and staff of the Department of English, University of Hyderabad; the UGC–DSA Special Assistance Programme of the Department of English, University of Hyderabad, for research and travel grants; the Sahitya Akademi (New Delhi); the Department of English and the Centre for Comparative Literature, University of Hyderabad; and the *Humanities Circle*, Central University of Kerala, for providing me forums to test my ideas and research findings.

I am grateful to Sanjukta Dasgupta, J.P. Das, Malashri Lal, Bidyut Mohanty, Manoranjan Mohanty, Uma Dasgupta, Kalpana Kannabiran, Jatindra K. Nayak, Himansu S. Mohapatra, Sumanyu Satpathy, late Brajanath Rath, Bauribandhu Kar, Phanindra Bhushan Nanda, S.M. Srichandan Singh, Arabinda Giri, Debendra K. Dash, Basanta K. Mallick, A.C. Pradhan, Meena Alexander, Omita Goyal, Amritjit Singh, and the anonymous reviewers of the manuscript for scholarly support.

Thanks also to the editorial team of Oxford University Press, India, for taking the project forward and seeing it through; Mr R. Nagarajan for ready assistance; and my family members at Bhubaneswar, Pondicherry, and Bhadrak for their moral support.

And finally, Simi, for being a good friend, and always, the first reader of all my writings.

Introduction

*It is indeed a subject of wonder that periodical publications should
have existed so long ... without having become subject to a regular
and systematic course of criticism.*

—James Mill (1824: 206)

In a digital age increasingly governed by e-publishing, the concept
of the periodical press/literature may appear somewhat arcane and
anachronistic. Indeed, when generic borderlines get blurred by the
new media, earlier practices related to information and cultural literacy must acquire new meaning or face obsolescence.

Earlier Trajectories

Periodical press/literature, in the sense in which it is understood
today, dates back to the heydays of the European Enlightenment.
Backed by the philosophy of John Locke, René Descartes, Joseph
Hartley, Immanuel Kant, and other Enlightenment thinkers,

periodical essayists tested the validity of ideas in the public domain. Initially aimed at shaping 'manners and morals', 'periodical essays', in due course, came to embrace a wide gamut of society and culture, reaching their peak during the nineteenth century. With the advent and consolidation of knowledge systems and disciplinary formations, especially in the university system, periodical literature acquired a new respectability and a canonical status.

Trust Money and a Leisured Class

What was the material base of this development? To begin with, industrial capitalism led to trust money and created a leisured class. Various societies devoted to different branches of learning sprang up along with respective journals to disseminate new thinking based on research. As mercantile activities flourished at home and in the colonies, a new breed of company officials—British, French, Dutch, and others—became amateur or professional seekers of knowledge in subjects as far apart as architecture to Archimedes. The case of James Mill, the father of John Stuart Mill, who worked for the British East India Company and wrote the monumental *The History of British India* (1817) in several volumes, is common to many colonial rulers who straddled the empire in various parts of the world. The Royal Asiatic Society, or its Bengal counterpart, conducted its annual research activities through journals which became an invaluable archive for academic professionals and administrators in course of time.

While the term 'periodical' may lend a special meaning to the writings of a professional thinker or an academic, it covers a wide range, bringing in magazines, journals, and newspapers. Periodicity is common to all the three. While newspapers primarily dealt with information and news, journals, and magazines did so through articles, essays, and notes carrying opinion that is the most contemporary treatment of an event or an issue. Periodical literature thus became the best forum to see the evolution of thought or opinion on a given topic. There were newspapers proper, weekly reviews, reviews in quarterlies, monthly magazines, and weekly journals. General periodicals came to be known as magazines. Popular in approach, such periodicals used shorter articles for a non-specialized or non-technical audience. Differences in this sense may be seen in terms of categories such as popular, trade news, and scholarly. A survey of periodicals during the nineteenth century shows the rise of trade periodicals that contained shorter articles and were aimed at professionals endowed with insights about commerce and the service industries. Scholarly periodicals, on the other hand, are seen to contain a higher level of technical terms and vocabulary, and followed a more complex conversation, recalling an earlier treatment of a topic or research area.

During the Victorian era, periodical literatures encompassed a great variety stretching from the more highbrow quarterlies such as the *Quarterly Review*, the *Edinburgh Review*, and the *Westminster Review* along with the cheaper 'penny dreadful', those aimed at family readership such as *Lloyd's Weekly Newspaper*, Charles Dickens's *Household Words*, and those meant for the middle-class readers such as the *Cornhill* and *Once a Week*. Some like the *Strand* used photographic illustrations for more specialized readers.[1]

Legacy: Past Continuous

A cursory look at the academic publishing and cultural scene today would reveal the legacy of the periodical literature and its continued presence in our midst. Periodicals are no longer limited to the print format. Many of them are published online, stored in distant database in forms like CD-ROM or other optical disc format. And yet, most such literature continues to appear in the periodical literature format. Specialist readers are no longer confined to the academic world or gentlemen administrators who combine the official task of governance with the pursuit of the intellect; they embrace increasingly a large body of lay readers who have access to an incredible storehouse of knowledge, thanks to the Internet and archives in the digital form. At the same time, the borderline between the hard-boiled academic with an arcane and esoteric vocabulary, and a more practical and level-headed bureaucrat administrator/policymaker has become more rigid. While research leading to periodical publications among mid-career administrators is not rare, it is not as common today as it used to be during the mid- or late nineteenth century. Why indeed should the rulers engage in research when with the click of a mouse they can have access to a database? On the other hand, serious research or writing by administrators, in India at least, seems to be relegated to the age of superannuation.

The continued influence of periodical literature is manifest more prominently in the academic discourse today, especially in the humanities and social sciences. Exploring the best and the latest in the given field through a literature survey, hypothesis, formulation of argument-backed evidence, in support and against, integral to the periodical literature article, has become a sine qua non for all research publications today. Adding to an existing body of knowledge has become a mandatory requisite in dissertations and scholarly publications. Scholars have turned their attention to the role of the media in the context of the nineteenth-century India. David Finkelstein and Douglas M. Peers's book, *Negotiating India in the Nineteenth-Century Media* (2000), serves as a good example of this trend.

Today the history of the Victorian periodical press is a genre in itself, a full-fledged area of study. There is a critical consensus that no aspect of the British literary–cultural history can be studied without reading the periodical press. Ever since the landmark publication of Walter E. Houghton's *The Victorian Frame of Mind* in 1957, the move to have an index of 40 to 50 leading periodicals gave way, in the course of time, to the most impressive *The Wellesley Index to Victorian Periodicals, 1824–1900* in five volumes.[2] The initial estimate of 16,000 titles published during this period has now been replaced by an unbelievably large number of 1,25,000 items. The Research Society for Victorian Periodicals organizes annual conferences and publishes the *Victorian Periodicals Review*.

The critical scene in India is a far cry. In most parts of the country, barring honourable exceptions such as Bengal and Kerala, there has not been sufficient effort to document, compile, and research the periodicals published in India during the Raj era. It must be remembered that the past is not a matter of relic; it has a continuous living presence in the entire gamut of our life. We would be destroying the remnants of this living past at our own peril. No area of our past deserves greater consideration than unravelling the history of the periodical press in neglected regions, including colonial Odisha. It is in this direction that we must go.

James Mill's exhortation for the study of the Victorian periodical press, underlined in the epigraph of this chapter, may well be extended to the study of periodical press in general as well for its varying impact on community building and nation formation in India.

The Context

The British arrived in Odisha officially in 1803, nearly a hundred years after they annexed Bengal for political and economic gains. It must be noted that the British rule in Odisha was an indirect one. For the most part, especially in the feudatory states and kingdoms—the so-called 'Gadjat' states—they ruled through political agents. In the coastal belt of Puri, Cuttack, Balasore, and Ganjam, called 'Mogalbandi', there was the zamindari system, much of which was controlled by Bengali owners, distantly located in Bengal and politically overseen by the local *gumasta* (agent) and the British officials posted at Cuttack, responsible for land revenue and the maintenance of law and order. The economy was in a shambles, as may be noticed from the writings of a sympathetic British official, G. Toynbee. The taxes that the British levied in colonial India varied from place to place, but the following extract may give a representative account of the situation prevailing in most parts of the country:

The taxes levied in different places varied with the idiosyncrasies of the Government or of the individual tax collector: but among them it may be noticed that people were mulcted for having houses to live in, or, if they had no houses, for their temporary sheds or huts. If they ate grain, their food was taxed at every stage in progress through the country; if they ate meat, they paid duty on it through their butchers. When they married, they paid for beating drums or putting up marquees. If they rejoiced at the set of Hindu festivals, they paid again; at the 'holi', for instance, on the red powder which they threw at each other; at the 'pala', on the ornaments which they tied to the horns of the cattle. Drinkers were mulcted by an exercise and smokers by a tobacco duty. Weavers, oil-pressers, fishermen, and such low-caste industrials, had as a matter of course to bear a special burthen. No house or slaves, or cattle could be sold, no cloth could be stamped, no money could be changed—even prayers for rain could not be offered, without payment on each operation of its special and peculiar tax. In short, a poor man could not shelter himself, or clothe himself, or earn his bread, or eat it, or marry, or rejoice, or even ask his gods for better weather, without contributing separately on each individual act to the necessities of the State! These were the regular taxes merely, and it certainly does not seem likely that any money could have slipped by owing to their want of comprehensiveness; but the revenue accounts of the times show that supplementary measures were occasionally found necessary to reach men who would otherwise have escaped. (Toynbee 2005: 43–4)

To what extent would the state of the economy have a bearing on the nature of the colonial modernity practised by the colonial state? The genesis of the first full-fledged journal in the region owes its existence to a mid-century economic crisis: *Utkal Dipika* arose, as we shall see, as a direct answer to the great famine of Odisha in 1866.

Colonial Modernity: A Contested Space

Just as the periodical press has become axiomatic for reading social and cultural history today, perhaps the same could be said regarding its link with colonial modernity. One must begin the exercise by admitting that there cannot be a uniform and consistent alignment between the vernacular press and the colonial modernity in India; the vast complexity in the historical situation does not permit such a unilinear approach. This modernity arguably came in a complex, contestatory, and ambivalent manner, and left lasting impressions on the political formations and the language communities.

The modernity propelled by the colonial state and its appendages rested upon the 'high modernism' of the European Enlightenment with its belief in the primacy of the West and the rhetoric of progress. In the subject nations and regions such as colonial Odisha, it produced various forms of resistance and acquiescence. One will, therefore, have to deal necessarily with the fractured relationships and the complex negotiations between the two. Again, resistance to colonialism came in the form of homegrown vernacular or alternative modernity among the emerging gentry. What was the nature of such modernity and how did it evolve over time? Critics like Satya P. Mohanty (2009) and others in recent times have underlined some of these developments in the domain of the nineteenth-century cultural history of India. Next, one will have to unveil the theoretical underpinnings while outlining the historical change recorded in the pages of the journals. And finally, we need to contextualize the periodical press and colonial modernity in the nationalist and regional frames adopted by cultural historians.

Twin Journals

While many periodicals played an important role, it is undoubtedly *Utkal Dipika* and *Utkal Sahitya* that occupy a pre-eminent place from the point of view of colonial/alternative modernity in the region. One will consequently have to look at the life of the founders of these two journals. By contextualizing the life and times of the journals and their editors, we could hope to illuminate a major aspect of colonial modernity.

Period of Study

The study begins with the year 1866 that marks the founding of the first major periodical following the killing famine in the same year; and we close the volume with the year 1936 that marks the formation of the separate province of Odisha. It would be rewarding to correlate the contents of the journals with the context of the ideology of colonial modernity.

The journals present an interesting study in themselves and we could pose the following questions regarding their growth and decline: What was the economic and political base of these two journals, their patronage systems and reception? What was the cultural and ideological background of the two editors, the evolution of their thinking as reflected in the pages of the journals? How were they implicated in the dominant ideologies of their times and how did they attempt to transcend them? How far did they succeed in their mission? How did the two journals respond to the question of editorial/literary freedom and censorship, questions dealing with gender and the nation, citizenship and sovereignty, colonial benevolence and the urge for self-rule? How did they influence public opinion? How did they bring in enlightened monarchs and administrators such as T.E. Ravenshaw and John Beames as part of their thinking? In striving for larger goals, did the two editors join hands, with journals beyond the 'borders'? How did they contribute to the making of the Odia sub-nationalism?

It is by framing the study against the backdrop of the above that we can hope to gain meaning about the periodical press and colonial modernity in Odisha.

Public Space

Colonial modernity manifests itself in a varied and insightful manner in the Indian public space. The Hindi public space would serve as a good example to discuss the trends in Hindi:[3] Vasudha Dalmia's pioneering work, *The Nationalization of Hindu Traditions: Bharatendu Harishchandra and Nineteenth-century Banaras* (1997), deals with the times and works of Bharatendu and the story of the Hindi public sphere in its nascent stage. Similarly, in *The Hindi Public Sphere (1920–1940): Language and Literature in the Age of Nationalism* (2009), Francesca Orsini takes the research forward and maps out transitions in the central preoccupations. Likewise, in *Periodical Literature in Colonial North India: Women and Girls in the Hindi Public Sphere* (2011), Shobna Nijhawan traces the emergence of women as a political subject which, at times, resists the master narratives of nationalist movements, such as the binaries of home and the world, purity and propriety, chaste sexuality, etc. On the other hand, in *Print and Pleasure: Popular Literature and Entertaining Fictions in Colonial North India* (2009), Francesca Orsini argues that while on the one hand print, under the impact of colonial modernity, advanced a public sphere that was chaste and purged of obscenity, as critics have argued, it simultaneously promoted an eclectic space for popular literature that celebrated taboos with great relish. Print did succeed in purging literature of Persian excess by implanting Sanskritized discipline, but it also led to easy dissemination of the bawdy tales of the *Qissa* tradition.

The Hindi public space during the colonial period outlined here is indicative of the trend. As we shall see in this book, colonial/alternative modernity in Odisha comes in the form of rich cameos. It encompasses a vast range: the question of interfaith dialogues, scientific and medical advancements, print cultures and colonial travel, emergence of the New Woman, religious chicanery in the monastery, merits and demerits of prohibition, medical ethics, vacation time in schools, and insurance policies. The list is endless and symptomatic of the complex and many-sided manner in which the periodicals reflect and refract colonial modernity.

Similarly, other volumes draw our attention to the role of the public space. A good example of this is *The Popular and the Public: Cultural Debates and Struggles over Public Space in Modern India, Africa and Europe* (2009), edited by Preben Kaarsholm and Isabel Hofmeyr. This volume shows how popular culture has shaped the public sphere, providing an alternative space for political debates in the nineteenth- and twentieth-century India, Africa, and Europe.

English education and the rhetoric of progress are the important flagposts that take the centre stage in the colonial discourse. The two editors and their contributors such as Fakir Mohan Senapati, Radhanath Ray, Chandramohan Maharana, and Radhanath Rao unmistakably stand for the *bhasha* tradition, buoyed by the efforts of sympathetic colonial masters such as T.E. Ravenshaw and John Beames. They internalize the editorial style of English periodicals and offer, in a self-reflexive manner, advisories to the readers to move in the desired direction and accept change as inevitable. For, 'changes are indeed desirable', declares *Utkal Sahitya*'s inaugural issue of 1897 and goes on to add:

Mankind cannot stand still in one place for ever. Immobility is anathema to a living and organic order. It is not the sign of wisdom to uphold tradition at the expense of change. Nor can we give up modernity for the sake of tradition. Only the wise know how to maintain a balance between the two. This is a path shown by wise men of ages and times ... As long as we remain alive, we will continue to follow this path. The treasure house of Odiya literature may not be overflowing with priceless valuables, but it is not empty either. There is a great need for a new literature. *Utkal Sahitya* seeks to act as a representative of both tradition and modernity.[4]

The notion of change as inevitable demands, according to editors like Biswanath Kar, a wise acceptance of the present (read the colonial rule); perhaps the only thing one could hope to do, suggests the subtext, is to come up with a form of response that preserves the cherished way of life, traditions, and life values of the subject-people while moving on with the times. In a varying manner, this refrain may sum up much of the response of the native elites in Odisha and elsewhere, before the emergence of militant nationalism in the first decades of the twentieth century in colonial Bengal.

Rhetoric of the Colonial State

The colonial state and its auxiliary units such as the missionary apparatus, for all their internal differences, created a system of education for the natives well-recorded by scholars in the field. The role of the missionaries including their Baptist counterparts in Serampore in Bengal, under the leadership of Carey, Marshman, and Ward, and the coming of the Orissa Mission Press, have been chronicled in the next chapter as part of the contextual reading. It is worth noting that 19 years after the British came to India, the first missionary schools were set up in Cuttack in 1822 (Mohanty 2005: 15–37).

Within the next one-and-a-half years, missionaries took up the management of 15 native schools in Odisha, including the English Charity School set up in 1823 in Cuttack which was taken over by the East India Company in 1841. Thanks to the printing of the Bible in the translation form (the New Testament was printed in 1809) and the widespread dissemination of missionary literature in Odia, several new genres such as the parable, morality play, miracle play, essay, novel, and tract came into being on the native soil.

Missionary narratives often rode on the back of the colonial state. In Odisha, the missionaries, Baptists from Serampore, and other denominations such as the Church of God, American Missionary Society, as auxiliary agents of the company/empire, consciously chose public space for conversion activities: temple premises, river ghats, festival celebrations, market areas, the Chariot Festival (*Ratha Yatra*, or the annual Car Festival in the temple town of Puri), and so on. The space was quickly turned into a makeshift battle zone of metaphysics and polemics, often a one-sided skirmish, given the fact that the 'warriors' from the other side that were targeted generally comprised poor and unlettered peasants, sundry men of town and curious onlookers, with a sprinkling of upper-caste men, whereas the preachers themselves came from a more privileged background, wore finer clothes, and were armed with printed tracts that showed the supremacy of the Christian faith vis-à-vis the vain idolatry of the native Hindus. Rev. C. Lacey's journal recordings (Dhall 1997: 110) give a typical sampling of a day's activities.

October 10 (1825): The weather has been fine today and I repaired to my old standing at Telengabazar [in Cuttack], and soon obtained a hundred hearers. I commenced with some men who were angling, and a by-stander soon enquired whether it was sinful to kill fish.

I attempted to show them what sin was, and a man cried that the Debtas [gods] would save them from their sins however great they might be.

Missionary: 'Brother, do you worship all the Debtas?'

Hindoo: 'Yes.'

Missionary: 'Brother, if you stand with one foot on one boat, and the other on another boat, what will be the result?'

People: 'Ah, he will be drowned in the middle.'

Missionary: 'You have many Debtas, and how can you tell from which to expect salvation? See, they are all divided, but you are leaning upon all, and so like a man in two boats you are sure to fall between. But if you worship Brahma (the great God), whom I preach to you, like a man in one good boat who arrives at the opposite shore, so you will be sure to find salvation, but learn from the man and the two boats, not to worship more than one God. I preach to you one Savior, and whosoever believes in him shall not perish, but have everlasting life.'

* * *

November 24 (1825): In the evening I carried on the war in the Lal Bazar with Mussulmans and Hindoos. Spoke of Christ as the only Savior and the Mussulmans ran away with their ears stopped, crying out 'Hear not that, Mahommet and Alla! Mahommet and Alla!' However, the Hindoos stood and heard the comparative merits of Christ and the Debtas: and several of the Brahmuns departed without answering, which not a little strengthened our cause in the eyes of the Soodras, many of whom are well able to appreciate the merits of this case. Several Europeans passed; one stood and heard about twenty minutes. To attempt to make Christians of Hindoos appear strange to them. However, by the foolishness of preaching, God will save them who believe; and we have no objections to being reckoned fools for Christ's sake and the gospels.

In the first episode, recorded with a sense of self-satisfaction regarding the day's work for the Lord, the missionary–preacher begins with a band of fishermen and bystanders, and soon involves them into a catchy conversation, punctuated by metaphors of 'angling' and 'boats' they could relate to. This is apparently 'home ground' for the preacher as well. For, the biblical allusion to the parable of Christ as the 'big fisherman' and the pious laity is unmistakably there, and the missionary can be expected to harness this in a strategic manner. Further, the idea of 'standing' 'with one foot' between 'two boats' is an alluring and convincing figure of speech native to fishermen that could not be refuted. Once the attention is held, the preacher introduces the idea of one God as the 'protector'. The idea of 'Brahma' is then wrongfully and cleverly slipped in, for this is a term that the native Hindus could be expected to understand and internalize. An alien concept to Christianity, the notion of 'Brahma', the supreme God of the Hindus, would powerfully appeal to the impressionable minds in the gathering. The idea of the preacher as the trickster underlies the entire discourse.

In the second episode, we see a relatively greater degree of difficulty in the rhetoric of conversion: The presence of Muslims and caste Hindus, especially Brahmins and Shudras, is acknowledged. The Muslims are portrayed as obdurate who 'ran away with their ears stopped' and the Brahmins 'left without answering'. The stereotyping of both the constituents is perfect. The acts of 'departures' are both physical and epistemological, deliberately cited so as to underline the irrefutability of the missionary position. The Europeans are shown as bystanders who are curious and amused, for they seem to be neutral to the situation, and have little stake in the outcome of the encounter. On the other hand, the preacher–diarist must convince himself of the worthwhileness of his own position by being self-righteous about his mission, and thus the concluding statement comes as an act of self-assurance: '...we have no objections to being fools for Christ's sake and the gospels.'

It is not my case that the missionary position inevitably merged with that of the colonial administration. In fact, there were many dissonances, and the two groups often had a conflictual relationship. What is common to both, and this fact is underlined in the given diary note, is the overarching narrative of 'salvation', both secular and spiritual, by following the chosen path of colonial modernity, based on the primacy of the West.

Female Education

Education, especially female education, was favoured by the missionaries. By 1850, a number of Baptist missionary schools were set up in

Balasore and Cuttack. In 1834, Mrs Lacey, the wife of the missionary earlier referred to, wrote approvingly to a female friend:

There never was such a hope-filled field of labor for a missionary wife as now among the native female Christians and their children. The women are all learning to read as well as the children and some of each [*sic*] read and understand their New Testament very well indeed. One of the female scholars is about 50 years of age and she is nearly ready to be put into the Testament class. (Sutton 1850: 254)

The acts of benevolence and self-validation we see in the letter of Mrs Lacey and her colleagues were held up for special praise in the British Parliament and considerably reduced the criticism against the company for causing economic misery among the native population. The Odia periodicals, in turn, were a fertile ground to debate the advance of education, especially female education. While full-fledged debates such as between Dwijendralal Roy, popularly known as D.L. Roy, and Rabindranath Tagore, and Bipin Chandra Pal and Tagore/ Pramatha Chaudhuri regarding the making of the New Woman in Bengal was to await the next century, a generally negative approach to female education was manifest in some of the early periodicals recorded in the next chapter. As the *Young Bengal* spokesman, Kalashchandra Basu, puts it trenchantly on 14 August 1846 while speaking at the Medical College Theatre, Calcutta (now Kolkata), 'on the education of Hindu females': 'She must be refined, reorganized, recast, regenerated' (Ray 1975: 198).

The New Woman

Bankim Chandra Chatterjee's essay 'Prachina Ebang Nabina' (The Old and the New) published in *Bangadarshan* becomes a pivotal reference point in the context of the New Woman. While the hardworking Prachina is held up for praise, Nabina, the new, is satirized. Rabindranath's espousal of the 'new' in all areas of life, including the gender, is also seen in his opposition to Chandranath Basu whose claims of Hindu scriptural supremacy fly in the face of misogynistic social practices, including child marriage, the lack of female education, and polygamy.

Similarly, the debate between Rabindranath Tagore and D.L. Roy stages the conflict between individual choice integral to empowerment versus wifely duties. In appropriating themes and legends from the Mahabharata such as that of Arjuna and Chitrangada and lending them a feminist turn in his verse play called *Chitrangada*, Tagore stood clearly on the side of the New Woman. Similar debates are also seen between the poet and Jitendralal Basu, the issue in question being the role assigned to the mother in Bengali literature/culture.

Equally instructive for us is the debate between Rabindranath and Bipin Chandra Pal that unfolded in the journal *Narayan*, founded by Chittaranjan Das, and Tagore's close friend and admirer Pramatha Chaudhuri's journal *Sabuj Patra*. Tagore's 'Streer Patra' (The Wife's Letter) appeared in *Sabuj Patra* in 1914 and Bipin Chandra Pal's 'Mrinaler Patra' (Mrinal's Letter) in the opening issue of *Narayan*. Bipin Chandra's treatment of the subject is viewed through 'the mocking masculine eyes of protecting relatives' (Dasgupta et al. 2013).

In Odisha, by the first half of the twentieth century, the concept of the New Woman was being debated in *Utkal Sahitya*, *Mukura*, and other journals by Sailabala Das, Sarala Devi, and Pratibha Devi on the one hand, and the champions of the 'advice for women' texts, such as Jagabandhu Singh on the other.

In the hands of a sympathetic Fakir Mohan, the tables are often turned. We see this in the novelist's hilarious tale, 'Patent Medicine', where a habitually drunk and disloyal husband, Babu Chandramani Patnaik, profligate and morally dissolute, learns the lesson of his life when he is given a thrashing with a broom by his wife, Sulochana Dei, with the full approval of the narrator. As he observes: 'Instead of the usual quarrels, both of them are now found engrossed in talking and reading books. They read *Utkal Sahitya*, *Mukura*, *Utkal Dipika*, and the newspapers.' He offers the final advice: 'If any beauty's husband has been unfortunately affected by this malady, the author makes a sincere request that the "patent medicine" could be tried for once.'[5] In this domestic story of crime and punishment, the deviant husband not only gets his just due, but he must also expiate by reading the literary periodicals of the times. Repentance must be shown not just in moral terms; due amends must also be made in intellectual and cultural terms, an unexpected tour de force.

The concern for a girl's education, in turn, was captured poignantly in the poem by Sushila:

> *What use is schooling for girls?*
> *Our countrymen ask:*
> *Isn't women's lives meant for family duties alone?*
> *If learned they shall not go*
> *for sure*
> *to 'Kutcheries' for service.*
> *But will roam around*
> *in unkempt hair....* [6]

Sushila's cry, symbolic of her generation, fell on deaf ears, and female education for a large section of the population would await a more propitious time in the future, given society's attitude to child marriage, female infanticide, and other regressive practices. Education for women had a limited mandate in the hands of the colonial administration, and such education was largely confined to upper-class Hindus and a sizable chunk of the Christian population in Odisha.

Conduct Book Tradition

Male resistance to women's education was persistent and obdurate. Jagabandhu Singh's widely circulated *Grihalaxmi* would question the merits of female education in the best of the 'conduct book' tradition. Although pertaining to a later period, it typifies an attitude common to the well-established misogyny in society.

It is true that Hindu women so far have not succumbed to the lure of *Alaxmi*. One must ponder, however, whether higher education currently imparted to women would make the continued worshipping of Laxmi possible. The day the Hindu woman refuses to accord respect to the household ideal that will surely be the beginning of Alaxmi.[7] (1946: ii; translation mine)

It would be seen that the conduct book promotes a largely patriar-
chal agenda; it takes recourse to clever means for pushing in an ideology of female containment.

> Presented in the conversational mode between an older male figure with
> authority and power, and a younger spouse 'willing' to learn, the outcome is left
> little in doubt. It must be remembered that the internalization of the second-
> ary status for the woman/wife takes place at the domestic site, which is per-
> haps one of the few private spaces left for the young wife. The space contains
> simultaneously an outlet for carrying out intimate intellectual, emotional, and
> physical/sexual interaction between the spouses. Thereby, it becomes a vital
> site for shaping the 'rightful' female behavior and wifely conduct. (Mohanty
> 2008: 46)

English education comes Janus-faced to the native gentry. The best
of the response, as we shall see later, went beyond mere acquiescence
to questioning the dominant paradigms and programmatic action by
the colonial state and administration. Where the subjugated could not
respond on equal terms, they deployed the mode of irony and sarcasm
as weapons. This is best expressed by Fakir Mohan Senapati through
prose and poetry in *Utkal Sahitya*. Here is Fakir Mohan's narrator in
Six Acres and a Third (*Chha Mana Atha Guntha*) mimicking the style
and claims of the British historian James Tod:

> There was only one pond in Gobindapur, and everyone in the village was used
> to it. It was fairly large, covering ten to twelve batis [a traditional unit of mea-
> surement], with banks ten to twelve arms-lengths high, and was known as
> Asura Pond. In the middle once stood sixteen stone pillars, on which lamps
> were lighted. We are unable to recount the true story of who had it dug, or
> when. It is said that demons, the Asura, dug it themselves. That could well be
> true. Could humans like us dig such an immense pond? Here is a brief history
> of Asura Pond by Ekadusia, the ninety-five-year-old weaver.
> The demon Banasura ordered that the pond be dug, but did not pick up
> shovels and baskets to dig it himself. On his orders, a host of demons came
> one night and did the work. But when day broke, it had not yet been com-
> pleted: There was a gap of twelve to fourteen arms-lengths in the south bank,
> which had not been filled in. By now it was morning, and the villagers were

already up and about. Where could the demons go? They dug a tunnel connecting the pond to the banks of the river Ganga, escaped through it, bathed in the holy river, and then disappeared. During the Baruni festival on the Ganga, the holy waters of the river used to gush through the tunnel into the pond. But, as the villagers became sinful, the rivers no longer did this. English educated babus, do not be too critical of our local historian, Ekadusia Chandra. If you are, half of what Marshman and Tod have written will not survive the light of scrutiny. (2006: 21–2)

The point is simple: if one were to accept unquestioningly the 'historical truths' peddled by James Tod without the need for verification of 'facts' of the empirical kind just because he, as an Englishman, enjoyed a celebrity status, then why should the ninety-five-year-old local historian Ekadusia's claim be discarded and treated as outlandish? In any case, it is now well known that a great deal that Tod wrote about the kingdoms of Rajasthan was garnered by fancy.

Fakir Mohan, as the narrator, however, is not primarily interested in the truth value of the historical claims. By parroting the sanctified 'historical' method, listing items and building an inventory such as the following: 'covering ten to twelve batis', 'with banks, ten to twelve arms-lengths high', 'gap of twelve to fourteen arms-lengths in the south bank', etc., and casually slipping in the remark—'we are unable to recount the true story of who had it dug'—as part of contrapuntal reading, he punctures the Western pretension to knowledge and unveils the possibility of an alternative epistemology.

New Historiography/Oral History/Local Tradition

The parody and the satire here are not just against the empirical claims of the English historians Marshman and Tod, but more crucially against the 'English-educated babus' who must constantly imitate a derivative discourse. Fakir Mohan's local historian is deliberately modelled after a humble Ekadusia Chandra (the name in Odia is meant to provoke laughter). The critique is against historiography based on rationally verified accounts of 'truth' to be seen against the claims of the local/oral history tradition which would gain acceptance much later in the West. In so doing, Fakir Mohan seems to pose a challenge to the dominant modernity project and offer an alternative modernity/epistemology.

The menace of the Western modernity finds recurrent mention in *Chha Mana Atha Guntha* that was serialized in *Utkal Sahitya* and had an enormous mass appeal.[8] Talking about the Asura Pond before the women appeared, Fakir Mohan's narrator declares in a tongue-in-cheek manner:

There is another equally irrefutable proof to support this contention that [there are fish in the pond]. Look over there! Four Kaduakhumpi birds are hopping about like Gotipuas, like traditional dancing boys. The birds are happy and excited because they are able to spear and eat the little fish that live in the mud. Some might remark that these birds are so cruel, so wicked that they get pleasure from spearing and eating creatures smaller than themselves! What can we say? You may describe the Kaduakhumpi birds as cruel, wicked, Satanic or whatever else you like; the birds will never file a defamation suit against you. But don't you know that among your fellow human beings, the bravery, honor, respectability, indeed, the attractiveness of an individual all depend upon the number of necks he can wring?

Some sixteen to twenty cranes, white and brown, churn the mud like lowly farmhands, from morning till night. This is the third proof that there are fish in the pond. A pair of kingfishers suddenly arrives out of nowhere, dive into water a couple of times, stuff themselves with food, and swiftly fly away. Sitting on the bank, a lone kingfisher suns itself, wings spread like the gown of a mem-sahib. Oh, stupid Hindu cranes look at these English kingfishers, who arrive out of nowhere with empty pockets, fill themselves with all manner of fish from the pond, and then fly away. You nest in the banyan tree near the pond, but after churning the mud and water all day long, all you get are a few miser-able small fish. You are living in critical times now; more and more kingfishers will swoop down on the pond and carry off the best fish. You have no hope, no future, unless you go abroad and learn to swim in the ocean. (2006: 21–2)

Here is Fakir Mohan at his best parodying English logic and legal-ese used in abundance to get even with the native populace. A suitable warning is held out by the narrator to be watchful lest one is stripped at any time of one's rightful claims. That the whole discourse comes in the guise of humour and sarcasm does not minimize the seriousness of the situation. The image of the pond and its denizens on the lookout for life and liberty stands as an objective correlative to the British rule.

English Language and the Rhetoric of Progress

The same logic is used to show complicity between the English language and the rhetoric of progress. In Fakir Mohan's iconic tale 'Dakamunshi' (The Postman),[9] we see the primacy of the English language that militates against the indigenous knowledge system in the late nineteenth century Odisha.

Social villains, morally renegade and ethically reprehensible are shown ... using the English language. At such times the English language becomes both threatening and menacing, upsetting the virtues of the traditional social order. Its secular, scientific, and modernizing role underlined by many colonizers is seen here as entailing a violation of the public ethic, thereby critiquing the notion of progress. (Mohanty 2000: 68)

In this classic story of the sacrifice of Hari Singh, the widower–postman, for his son Gopal, who gets the coveted job of a postmaster, thanks to his acquisition of the English language, we see not only the cruel act of betrayal of the father by his son, but more crucially, the defeat of the familial and indigenous in the hands of the alien tongue and way of life. This is a theme prominently found in the journal *Pradipa*, established in 1885 (see Chapter 1). While Gopal, the profligate son, showers 'English blows' upon his unlettered father and bundles him out of the house unceremoniously in the middle of the wintry night, because the old man's coughing is a source of embarrassment to the visiting memsahib, the 'native' peon comes to the rescue, since he has a 'native' heart. It is the latter that wins the wholesome approval of the narrator. In this Manichean world of good and evil, reminiscent of the New England narratives, it is perhaps wit and humour that can ensure the survival of the dispossessed.

The dialectic between the 'modern' and the 'traditional' is incessantly played out in Fakir Mohan's story 'Dakamunshi'. While the 'modern' comes threatening the life values of a living community, the primordial is a source of welcome refuge. We may, therefore, conclude:

In the course of the story, the graded reiteration of the word, the term 'English' not only denotes the language as distinct from the vernacular, not only refers to the new western or English education, but also acquires connotations of an alien and arrogant set of attitudes and values. It speaks of the sharpness of Fakir Mohan Senapati's ideological vision that through his incisive social realistic narratives such as 'Dakamunshi' he offered a critique of the discourse of power based on language dialectics. (Mohanty 2000: 73)

It would thus be seen that colonial modernity in Odisha comes in a complex and many-sided manner through the medium of the periodical press. This modernity works pre-eminently through the colonial state and its agencies; at other times, it meets with resistance and in the hands of the astute, typically through subversive irony, leads to vernacular/alternative modernity.

In Odisha, colonial modernity came in the form of a contested space through markers such as historiography, Western medicine, female education, English language, and the rhetoric of progress.

In the next chapters we shall review the history of the periodical press in Odisha, the life and times of two of the notable editors, and examine colonial/alternative modernity in the twin journals before coming to conclusions.

Notes

1. See www.oxfordbibliographies.com/view/document
2. See www.victorianweb.org
3. I am grateful to Gautam Chaubey for his insights in the area.
4. All translations, unless otherwise indicated, are by me.
5. 'Patent Medicine', Utkal Sahitya, 17th Year, 7th Issue, September 1913.
6. My translation of a poem by Sushila, a student of Mission Girls' School, Cuttack. The poem originally appeared in Utkal Dipika, 13 June 1885. Also quoted (with an alternate translation of the same poem) in Pradhan (1988).

7. See also Walsh (1995).

8. A crowd reportedly gathered in the court premises at Cuttack believing that the evil-doer Ramachandra Mangaraj would be tried for his crimes. This was reported in the novel in a serialized form in *Utkal Sahitya*.

9. Extracts quoted by me are translated by me from *The Stories of Fakir Mohan Senapati* (1991). 'Dakamunshi' originally appeared in *Mukura*, 7th Year, No. 6, September 1912.

1

The Rise of the Periodical Press in Odisha

> *Good Lord! The man without whom Hari would have perished in early life and without whose support he would have begged in the street, that hapless father has suddenly become an old servant! Long live education, long live development!*
>
> —*Pradipa*, August 1885

The refrain about filial ingratitude thanks to baneful English education finds several echoes in many Odia journals, including *Pradipa*, towards the close of the nineteenth century. The practice would have entirely surprised an earlier generation unused to the growing power and outreach of the periodical press. Fakir Mohan must have used many such sources in his masterly depiction of characters in tales like 'Dakamunshi', discussed in the 'Introduction' to this volume.

In this chapter, we shall survey the history of the periodical press in Odisha. While much of it will be in the form of a historical review of the narrative kind, efforts will be made, wherever possible, to comment on the emerging trends and recurrent patterns. It is a background chapter that will give some idea about the growth and decline of periodical literature in Odisha to the interested readers.

News archives during the Mogul period were preserved; such accounts by James Tod in 1828 may be seen in the Royal Asiatic Society, London. It contains news regarding the promotion and career records of government officials, visits of the king/emperor as well as royal edicts of news regarding military matters.[1] James Tod (20 March 1782–18 November 1835), born in London and educated in Scotland, served the East India Company as a military officer and political agent and is best known for his work *Annals and Antiquities of Rajasthan, or the Central and Western Rajput States of India* (1832). He offered in his accounts a somewhat idealized view of the life of the Rajputs, and advocated that the colonized territories such as Rajputana ought to have homogenous populations for their own welfare and better governance. As indicated in the 'Introduction', native writers such as Fakir Mohan Senapati often alluded to the work of Tod in an ironical manner in order to question the European claim to historical truth.

Early Days: British India

The first attempts at the circulation of news were made during the British rule in India. As Bauribandhu Kar (2013) records in his seminal study of the periodicals (I have based myself largely on Kar's study in this chapter), a group of disgruntled officials of the East India Company left the organization in 1777, and attempted to set up a newspaper under the leadership of William Bolts (Kar 1989 [2013]).[2] Bolts said that he had 'in manuscript many things to communicate which most intimately concerned every individual', but he was asked to quit Bengal and leave for Madras for an onward passage to England (1772: 528).[3] Later James Augustus Hickey, an Irishman, established a weekly named *Hickey's Bengal Gazette* in 1779. Hickey strongly criticized Governor General Warren Hastings and Lady Hastings. For his outspokenness, Hickey was imprisoned and his paper was auctioned. For his intrepid behaviour and steadfast championing of press freedom, he is rightly regarded today as the Father of the Indian Press.[4]

In 1780 appeared *India Gazette* under the leadership of Messnick and Read. It received some postal concession from the government. The *Calcutta Gazette* was published in 1784 under the full supervision of the government. Around the same time appeared the *Bengal Journal* and the monthly called the *Oriental Magazine*, or *Calcutta Amusement*. Soon after, in 1786 appeared the newspaper called the *Calcutta Chronicle*. Most newspapers remained prudently conformist after witnessing the punishment meted out to Hickey. (The British Library in London has an impressive collection of the early English-language Indian newspapers.)[5] By 1880, several periodicals appeared, chief of which were the *Madras Courier* (1785), *Madras Gazette* (1798), and *Bombay Herald* (1789) whose name was changed to *Bombay Gazette* in 1791. These were primarily in English.

Periodical press dealing with literature, culture, religion, philosophy, and education gained ground in the regional context during the nineteenth century. The publication of such literature was facilitated during the rule of Lord Hastings. The pioneers in this direction were G.S. Buckingham, Raja Ram Mohan Roy and the missionaries. Raja Ram Mohan Roy and Bhabani Charan Banerjee jointly edited *Sambad Kaumudi*. Parting company from Roy, Bhabani Charan set up *Samachar Chandrika* in 1822. The same year Ram Mohan established a Persian newspaper called *Mirat-ul-Akhbar*. Through his forums, he propagated the abolition of sati, the regeneration of the Hindu society, and the introduction of Western education.

The missionaries, in turn, published several journals from Serampore such as the Bengali monthly *Dig Darshan* (1818) and the weekly *Samachar Darpan* (1818). *Dig Darshan* was primarily a mouthpiece of the missionaries, and disseminated news of nearly sixty new centres in Bengal; the periodical continued till 1840. During the reign of William Bentinck appeared several periodicals such as *Chandrodaya*, *Maha Darpana Bhaskara*, *Rasaraja*, *Gyanadarpana*, *Bangadoota*, *Sadhuranjana*, *Gyana Sancharini*, *Rangapur Bartabaha*, *Rasa Mudgar*, etc.

The first Urdu newspaper appeared in 1837. Syed Muhammad Khan, the brother of Sir Syed Ahmed, the founder of Aligarh Muslim

University, edited *Syed-ul-Akbar* in 1838. In due course were published *Fawadi Nazreen, Quaran-ul-Sadi, Banares Akhbar, Simla Akhbar*, and *Zia-ul-Akhbar*. Similarly, there were several publications in Persian such as *Jubat-ul-Akhbar* (1833) and *Suraj-ul-Akhbar* (1844). The first was ably edited by Munshi Wajid Ali Khan and was supported by the royalty of Bharatpur, Alwar, Hyderabad as well as other states and principalities.

The *Bombay Darpan* appeared both in English and Marathi in 1832. *Saptahik Prabhakar* was started in 1841. The American missionaries, on their part, took up several such as *Dininodaya* (1842), *Dininaprakash* (1849), *Dinina Bandhu* (1842), and *Indu Prakash* (1862).

The Hindi periodical press was led by Bharatendu Harischandra. The first Hindu journal, *Samachar Sudha Barshan*, appeared in 1854. Others followed: *Sabapakarak* (1861), *Bharat Khandaniruta* (1864), *Kavibachan Sudha* (1876), *Harischandra Magazine* (1874), and *Chandrika* (1874). Bharatendu Harischandra was the editor of *Kavibachan Sudha, Harischandra Magazine*, and *Chandrika*. Equally notable was the role of Balkrishna Bhatt in editing *Hindi Pradip* (1877).

Other languages such as Telugu, Malayalam, Gujarati, and Punjabi did not lag behind with journals such as *Karnataka Prakasika* (1865), *Bratanta Patrika* (1874), and *Satyanandan* (1884) being published. The missionaries spearheaded several journals such as *Hitabadi* in Bengali, *Bibekabardhini* in Telugu, *Swadeshi Mithran* in Tamil, *Sridarbar* (1867) in Punjabi, and *Surat Mitra* (1863) and *Desha Mitra* (1865) in Gujarati.

Print Literature: Role of the Missionaries in Odisha

Odisha had clearly lagged behind in this respect. The first newspaper to be circulated in the handwritten form was *Kujibara Patra*, edited by Sadhu Sundar Das of the Kujibara Math of Choudwar in the Cuttack district (Dash 1997: 4). Begun in 1822, it closed down by 1838. The first printed book in Odia on the other hand was the New Testament by the Baptist Missionary Society published in 1811 by the Serampore Missionary Press in Bengal. It was translated by William Carey and Purushram Pandit (Mohanty 1978: 2).[6] The Odia–English dictionary was published by Mohan Prasad Thakur.[7] M.P. Das (1984) gives a good account of the history of early Odia printing. Similarly, Amos Sutton's 1850 publication, *Orissa and its Evangelization*, illuminates our understanding of the missionary activities in Odisha.[8]

The Cuttack Mission Press was set up in 1837. *Gyanaruna*, edited by C. Lacey, appeared in 1849. *Prabodha Chandrika*, published in 1856, gave a great deal of courage to Odia language, literature, and culture apart from dealing with the missionary activities. Issue number 20 of the same journal, printed in Cuttack by W. Brooks, contained the following chapters: 'Words of Wisdom by Vishnu Sharma', 'About the Clouds', 'All About a Steamboat', 'Sea Horse', '*Samachar Patrika*', '*Utkal Panjika*' (the Almanac of Odisha), and 'In Search of Pearls on the Island of Ceylon'. *Prabodha Chandrika* may be considered the first news and literary magazine of Odisha (Mohanty 1978: 7).

In 1861, the Christian Vernacular Literature Society published a monthly named *Arunodaya*. The East India Company and the missionaries directly and indirectly pioneered the creation of the periodical press in India. Since most of these dealt primarily with missionary matters, Gourishankar Ray felt the need to bring out an independent news magazine in Odia.

Utkal Dipika (1866)

Utkal Dipika was first brought out on 4 August 1866 by the Cuttack Printing Company at Dargha Bazar. The company's board of directors comprised the following: Harekrishna Das, Jagmohan Ray, Bichitrananda Das, Dinanath Sarkar, Sudarshan Das, Lakshminarayan Rai Choudhury, Radhashyam Narendra, Gourishyam Jena, Golak Chandra Bose, Banamali Singh, and Gourishankar Ray who was the editor. The two auditors of the company were Jagabandhu Ghosh and Jaganmohan Lala.

Initially using stone letters, the press soon switched over to litho versions. The company started with 7,500 rupees as the capital investment and several prominent writers were stakeholders. *Utkal Dipika* was a major mouthpiece dealing with the cultural, literary, social, and economic life of the Odia-speaking people. It dealt primarily with the following aspects:

(a) The news of the various lands
(b) Details of education, culture, and national life
(c) Discussion about the Odia language and literature
(d) An account of the needs and problems of Odisha
(e) A list of holidays and the almanac of Odisha

Utkal Dipika dealt extensively with the news of different lands and people through prose, anecdotes, and poetry. For example, *Utkal Dipika's* additional issue number 16 that came out in November 1866, published a poem entitled 'Odishya Bilapa' that portrayed the plight of the Odias during the great famine of 1866.

Utkal Dipika collected most of its news from the British news magazines since Odisha did not have the source of teleprinters. Similarly, *Dipika* dated 29 December 1866 reported a serious accident in Amritsar taken from the *Educational Gazette*. Likewise, there was a good deal of news coverage regarding natural disasters, war, floods, cyclones, and famine. Although *Dipika* appeared only once a week, Gourishankar gave importance to news that spoke against the tyranny of the Raj.

Education, both English and Odia, formed an important aspect of *Dipika's* coverage. In its issue number 40, dated 6 February 1869, the journal reports:

It is learnt that the government has ordered the imparting of education through the medium of Odiya. ... We request the Director to implement the same system in all other schools as well. Nor was it unaware of the baneful aspects upon the youth of Odisha due to English education. After the opening of [the] high school in Cuttack, we began to think of the effect of the present system of education upon the youth of today and were plunged into the ocean of sadness. For, much was expected of this youth, but little realized. For the past twenty-five years or so, the government school has been set up and many products have gone out to Bengal for higher education. However, it is sad to note that aside from earning their livelihood, very few have been able to give any account of themselves. Further, being educated by public money, they are unable to carry out any public welfare ...

The only result so far has been that in many subdivisions, a good number of Clerks have been produced. Nothing more has been achieved. Few have cherished independence beyond the life of a Clerk. (p. 30)

Commending the efforts of Commissioner Ravenshaw, *Utkal Dipika* wrote: 'Our Commissioner Ravenshaw Sahib is greatly interested in education. It is generally known that this interest has been seen from his Patna days; the same was also noticed at the prize giving ceremony he addressed.' Gourishankar took special care to publish items related to education, at times by adding special print runs of *Utkal Dipika*. At the same time, there were many amusing reports about the habits and behaviour of Odias in *Dipika*. About the character of the Odias, it says:

The behavior and life style of the Odias is different from the others. Most of them are the followers of Hinduism. The upper castes have picked up some education. We do not think that they are wary of hard work or industry. They are endowed with intelligence and are in many respects trustworthy. They travel to Calcutta for work and become objects of praise for their behavior and conduct.[9]

Utkal Dipika played a crucial role in the preservation and promotion of the Odia language during the nineteenth century. Literary debates were extensively covered, just as books were regularly taken up for reviews. Radhanath, Madhusudan, Kamapal Mishra, and Ram Shankar Ray added their might in the form of literary criticism. Special attention was given to literary texts meant for study in the classroom context. The Letters to the Editor section was given particular importance and through such medium, the grievances of the common people were communicated to the British rulers. Memorandums were submitted to the government for grievance redressal. The list of holidays and details of religious rituals were regularly covered in its pages for nearly seventy years and it assumed a leading role in being a vehicle for the artistic and cultural life of Odisha. After Gourishankar, Rai Bahadur Sudam Charan Nayak took up its editing for a while.

Along with Gourishankar, mention must be made of Fakir Mohan Senapati for the introduction of the modern press in Odisha that would spearhead the promotion of the Odia language and literature. He formed an association comprising Babu Jayakrishna Choudhury, Bholanath Samantaray, Damodar Prasad Das, Radhanath Rai, and himself. The mission was clear:

Those who purchase the company's share will get much profit. The scriptures like Ramayana and Mahabharata, if printed, will sell at cheap rates. It would be much easier to read the printed books than the palm leaf manuscripts. It would not be necessary to call for special scripture readers. The boys can easily acquire learning. No outsiders can abuse the Odias as fools. (Behera and Dash 2000: 46)

They collected 1,200 rupees and formed a press company called P.M. Company & Co. The second-hand machine purchased from Midnapore Mission Press unfortunately did not function. Borrowing 800 rupees from Babu Kishori Mohan Das, a new Super Royal Columbian Press was purchased from Calcutta and brought to Balasore through a bullock cart. Patronage was given by the Balasore collectorate for printing of all the documents. With the profits, Fakir Mohan brought out *Bodha Dayini* and *Balasore Samadbahika*; the latter contained news items (Behera and Dash 2000: 51). It appeared in July 1869 as a monthly and became a fortnightly in 1872, and a weekly later in the same year.

Utkal Darpan (1873)

The journal first appeared in January 1873. Its advent was announced by Raja Baikuntha Nath Dey in the form of an advertisement in *Utkal Dipika*, dated 19 November 1872: 'We have decided to publish a monthly called *Utkal Darpan* [Giri 2007: 17–18]. Its main objectives are the improvement of Odiya literature and reforms of the social life of Orissa. Consequently, it will carry proposals dealing with education, literature, science, music, politics and society.'

After two years of its publication, that is, from 1875 it became a fortnightly and in 1877, it became a weekly. It ran well up to 1884 and was discontinued in 1885 when an author named Jangabandhu Banerjee wrote a critical piece against the government of Bengal.

While in circulation, the journal carried many pieces of very high standard. Poetry, prose, novels, essays, philosophy, politics, psychology, and textbooks—all of them were given sustained importance. It critiqued the *Bharatavarshara Itihasa* (The History of India)[10] by

Fakir Mohan Senapati on two grounds: firstly, on the charge that it was lengthy and followed the Bengali model, and secondly, that the historical account criticized the British and often used idiosyncratic poetry to depict historical figures and themes. This is a remarkable instance of the social history of the nineteenth century. The review of Fakir Mohan's historical account appeared in *Darpan*'s issue dated 15 July 1884. Life histories of great personalities were given prominence in *Utkal Darpan*. The lives of Surendranath Banerjee and Ram Mohan Roy appeared serially from 24 June 1883 and 8 June 1884 respectively. This model was then followed by later journals such as *Sikhyabandhu* and *Naba Sambad*.

Utkal Darpan brought together many amusing incidents from national and international domains. For instance, in its issue dated 2 July 1882 (p. 165), the journal reports that a married American woman gave a silk broom to her lady friend as a wedding gift so that it could be used if necessary. We see the treatment of this theme in Fakir Mohan's memorable tale 'Patent Medicine'. These are many such anecdotes narrated for the sake of an ethical life. In keeping pace with the changing times, in the later period greater coverage was given to health, agriculture, commerce, politics, and religion. Although *Darpan* established a reputation for itself, it was criticized by *Utkal Dipika* for being subject to Bengali influence and for committing grammatical errors.

Despite the passage of time, *Utkal Darpan* remains a pathfinder in the domain of Odia prose. Radhanath's '*Bibeki*' was first published here just as Madhusudan's '*Ulkapinda*' was discussed in its pages. The journal would remain an index of the literary–cultural life of the nineteenth-century Odisha.

Utkal Madhupa (1878)

A group of cultural-minded citizens of Cuttack set up an organization called Utkal Sabha in 1877 to discuss matters related to literature, culture, and religion. Following the suggestion of the playwright Ramshankar Ray, a journal called *Utkal Madhupa* was established in 1878 under the editorship of Krushna Mohan Patnaik. An announcement was made by Gopal Charan Dutt on behalf of Utkal Sabha in the following words:'It is brought to the notice of all that an eight page periodical named *Utkal Madhupa* is going to appear soon. The journal will, among other things, discuss the classical poetry of Upendra Bhanja and others as well as the works of recent poets and writers. The subscription cost is one and half rupees per year.' *Madhupa* began in April 1878 and became extinct in 1919. The average size of the journal comprised sixteen pages. *Madhupa,* in the first year, was edited by Gopal Charan Dutt, and in the second year, by Jogendra Narayan Bakshi.

The historical novel *Saudamini* appeared serially in this forum and made a great impact on the readers. Similarly, the debate over the merits of Upendra Bhanja and Radhanath originated in the pages of *Utkal Madhupa* (Acharya 2009: 27). The primary aim of *Utkal Madhupa* was to discuss classical literature, such as Upendra Bhanja's *Labanyabati* and *Koti Brahmanda Sundari.*

In the meeting of Utkal Sabha on 8 January 1878, Pyari Mohan Acharya, who was a guest speaker, spoke of the need to carve out a new literary path. The earlier tradition, he argued, has already exhausted itself.[11] Refuting this viewpoint, Chaturbhuja Patnaik suggested that the charge of obscenity may not be entirely true; it has to be seen in its context. On the other hand, classical literature also contains many worthy aspects that are not being adequately projected due to the negligence of the educational department.[12] The debate continued for quite some time in Utkal Sabha and much of it was reported in *Utkal Dipika.* A member of the audience wrote: 'Why are some people against classical poetry? Isn't it because of non-comprehension? Should the coconut be condemned because the monkey is unable to eat it?'[13] Clearly, *Utkal Madhupa* played a leading role in condemning the Bhanja literature. This aspect apart, the journal published many articles of very high standard such as the poem 'Jeebana Chuta', its translation by Kapileshwar Bidyabhushan and Pyari Mohan's 'Odishara Itihasa' (The History of Odisha).

Utkal Madhupa courted controversy by opposing the classical Bhanja literature. It was severely criticized by *Utkal Dipika* on this account. However, due to its new approach, style, and idiom, it became widely popular among a new readership and within a relatively brief span carved out a space for itself.

By 1878, major changes had come to Odia literature with a growing interest in Western literature through Bengali publications. By 1875, the Bengali essay had acquired an independent genre with leading practitioners such as Ram Mohan Roy, Kashinath Tarkapanchanan, Gourikanta Bhattacharya, Krishnamohan Bandapodhyaya, Rajendralal Mitra, Rangalal Bandopadhyaya, Rajnarayan Basu, Pyarichand Mitra, Kaliprasanna Singh, Dwijendranath Tagore, Kaliprasanna Ghosh, and Bankim Chandra Chatterjee.

The influence of Brahmo Samaj is extensively felt in the three journals: *Bangadarshan*, *Utkal Madhupa*, and *Pradipa*. Akshay Kumar Datta wrote many essays on science in the Bengali periodical press. Gradually, the Bengali influence disappeared and acquired an Odia identity. We may see this evolution from 'Bibeki' and 'Kalidas' of *Utkal Darpan* to 'Samskara' and 'Bandhuta' of *Pradipa*. The impact is felt in later journals like *Utkal Sahitya* and *Mukura*. *Madhupa* dealt with a wide variety of literary genres: essays dealing with history, biography, social reforms, science, education and psychology, poetry based on spirituality and nature, and other genres such as popular literature, novels, short stories, criticism, and reviews.

Pradipa (1885): Colonial Critique

Pradipa's first edition, printed by the Cuttack Printing Company, came out in January 1885. From the second edition onwards, the printer and publisher was Sarat Chandra Mukhopadhyaya. The defining feature of the journal was a column called 'Mathara Sambad' (News from the Monastery), a unique feature that centre staged in every issue the bane of drinking and debauchery, a corrupt and decadent life associated with 'English education'.

In the January 1885 episode, for instance, we see the curious case of Dharma Das Babaji (a pun on the word 'dharma'). India is on the path of 'development', and there is fondness of the English-educated class for drinking and visiting brothels. The young boy Madhab reads Mill, Darwin, and Spenser regularly and turns to scepticism—'I am a sceptic, I am a sceptic!' he proclaims constantly. Social science taught him that it is not improper to visit the brothel for the sake of health; indeed, it is salutary to do so. It has the sanction of science. Madhab is afflicted by a venereal disease. One day he and his student meet each other accidentally in a drunken state. Others save the couple from a scuffle.

In the February 1885 issue of *Pradipa*, there is more news from the monastery. The episode depicts the relationship between science and religion. Ramesh Babu pontificates on many issues, lectures widely about the need not to marry before the age of 25, but does so at 22. He takes to liquor and frequents brothels. He acquires a family of two children and a wife, and dies prematurely due to heart attack. The columnist tells us blithely that this is the second step towards 'development!'

In the April 1885 issue, compounder Kedarnath is shown working in the hospital for Gajendra Babu. Kedar steals medicine casually from the shelves and becomes the doctor of Gobindapur. Owning the 'Grand Medical Hall', he develops an illicit relationship with a young widow, and later the wife of a religious-minded man of Gobindapur, named Biswanath Babu. A victim of sexual assault, the wife ends her life. The moral of the story is that such religious imposters are everywhere in India these days, thanks to the new education sweeping the country.

The July 1885 'News from the Monastery' captures the life of Baishnab Charan Patnaik, the son of Harihar Patnaik of Aswapur. The episode shows the evil of anglicization and Westernization. Baishnab ignores his father and takes care of his father-in-law. 'The more the English "juice", the juice of new civilization, enters his stomach, the more Baishnab becomes a "reformer" of society.' His mentor is a classmate named Nabinakrushna Gupta. Both of them move in together and join the Intermediate in Arts (IA) course in the college. Soon, Baishnab gets initiated into the 'new life.' 'Take half a glass of brandy regularly for the sake of your health,' he is told. In due course, liquor and prostitutes become a regular habit with Baishnab. Visiting his village he must shake hands with the village women and folks. He removes his shoes and bows down to anyone. He is upset with his wife who does not put on a gown, and instead puts on a sari. The villagers take him to be a Christian. Baishnab leaves home, forsakes his Hindu parents, and goes in search of the promised land of Western culture. The narrator asks pointedly, 'Is this the result of English education?' He muses: 'Seeing the life of Nabina and Baishnab, I have little doubt that the "salvation" of India is not too far away! This must be "the fourth step in India's development".' The novelist Fakir Mohan Senapati who wrote the memorable tale 'Dakamunshi' as a classic parable of English education may have been influenced by this column.

And finally in the August 1885 issue of *Pradipa*, the narrator tells of a letter he receives from Calcutta. We hear the story of Harihar Babu Deputy. His parlour is decorated with a tea pot placed at the centre; a sofa adorns the room, there are pictures of memsahibs on the wall but, alas, no sign of any deity, gods, or goddesses! Inside the house sits a woman in traditional attire chanting the name of Hari. The brown sahib who enters the house calls out: 'Hello Haribabu, who is this old fool spoiling your mattress?' The Deputy Babu replies: 'Oh, he is an old servant of our family and takes much liberty, you know!'

The narrator reflects: 'Good Lord! The man without whom Hari would have perished in early life and without whose support he would have begged in the street, that hapless father has suddenly become an old servant! Long live education, long live development!' The Babu and Hari spend time together drinking and end the party with three cheers. Inside, Hari's idle wife complains against her mother-in-law and begs to be sent back to her parents' place. Early next morning, Harihar promptly sends his parents away. Such disputes, the narrator concludes sardonically, are not few in number. Who can deny that the law is not 'progressing'? Surely be the fifth step of India's 'development'! The Western education is a double-edged sword, seems to be the refrain in many of the periodicals in colonial Odisha, as indeed in the rest of the country.

Sikhyabandhu (1885): New Education

Several events of cultural and political significance took place in 1885. The Indian National Congress was founded in this year. There was an improvement in the printing technology. The journals *Sanskarak* and *Sebak* became weeklies. Two monthly periodicals *Pradipa* and *Sikhyabandhu* were published. Hailing these events as noteworthy, *Utkal Dipika* expressed satisfaction and a sincere hope that the journals and in particular *Sikhyabandhu* would be patronized by the Odia society.[14] The prophecy came true and the journal became a major forum to carry out debates over textbooks. An announcement made by Jogendranath Jena, Secretary, Kaligali, Cuttack, on 1 January 1885 soon appeared in *Utkal Dipika*'s issue dated 20 January and 3 January 1885 (p. 7): 'In the next three weeks, a monthly periodical called *Sikhyabandhu* is going to be published. It would be particularly useful to the students and teachers. A group of qualified teachers have agreed to contribute to this journal. It is an eight page periodical whose annual subscription including postage is one rupee per year.'

From the very beginning, *Sikhyabandhu* played a pioneering role in bringing the teachers and students together. It commended the work of Radhanath, the joint inspector of schools, and attempted to cover up many of the alleged irregularities in the selection of textbooks that Radhanath was accused of. *Utkal Dipika* was forthright in its views and stated that the journal ought not to lavish unqualified praise upon Radhanath. For otherwise, the readers would conclude that *Sikhyabandhu* was unnecessarily interested in singing the praise of the education department.[15]

Many of the published pieces in *Sikhyabandhu* did not carry the names of the authors and such anonymous articles were remarkable in their content and style. The journal threw light on the contemporary approach to the teaching of literature. It regretted that for the most part, the teaching of language or literature was confined to vocabulary and syntax. It seldom touched upon crucial aspects such as emotions, thought processes, and composition underlying the literary texts.

Most teachers regrettably became content if their students managed to pick up a few words along with their synonyms and antonyms. For, they themselves may not be aware of the overall significance of the text, content as they were with the glossary and grammar. Teachers were seldom drawn to the topic or the authors, the nature of the composition, its historical and cultural setting, and the merits and demerits of the language used. Similarly, the periodical discussed textbooks related to literature, grammar, healthcare, geography, and so on. It evoked strong emotions among its supporters like Radhanath Ray.

Apart from Radhanath Ray and Madhusudan Rao, others who contributed to *Sikhyabandhu* included Lalit Mohan Chakraborty, Bholanath Das, Raghunath Mishra, Prabhakar Sharma, and Sarat Chandra Mukopadhyaya. There were many insightful discussions on contemporary religious, mythological, and literary topics. The journal imparted a close reading of the literary texts and focused attention on content and style. It may thus be correct to state that such practical criticism later associated with the New Critics and I.A. Richards, was attempted for the first time in the pages of *Sikhyabandhu*. From 1887 onwards, the journal assumed a new name as *Naba Sambad* and became a weekly. In its issue dated 3 January 1885 (p. 98), it announced that Babu Bhupatinath Bose and Sadhu Charan Ray would become its editors.

Naba Sambad (1887): Nationalist Discourse— the Beginnings

This journal appeared on 23 January 1887. While some considered it a sequel to *Sikhyabandhu*, the editor himself declared it to be an entirely new publication with a fresh set of aims and objectives. The fee for its annual subscription was one-and-a-half rupees. The composition by Madhusudan Rao heralded the periodical as a vehicle for the new age, carrying the nationalistic spirit involving the many linguistic and cultural constituents of the Indian nation. It vowed to abolish superstition, corruption, misdeeds, and illiteracy, and usher in a new climate of nationalistic fervour. The journal continued to publish high-calibre articles and essays dealing with textbooks, prose, and poetry. It critiqued many textbooks in currency at the high-school level and considered them inappropriate for the children of a certain age.[16] It excelled in the publication of the reviews of some of the most notable books and publications of the period such as *Sati Natakara Samalochana*, dated 13 February 1887, and *Nandi Keshwari Samalochana*, dated 17 November 1887. It published serially the travelogues of Radhanath Ray. It ridiculed the idle habits of the English-educated youth of the period, addicted to wine, women, and parasitical living. It described the decadence that had set in the contemporary society. The Brahmo movement then divided into two—Sadharan Brahmo Samaj (1878) and Naba Bidhan (1880)—was discussed extensively in the pages of the journal. The editor not only published news items but invariably gave his own interpretations too. For instance, in the issue dated 31 March 1886 (p. 36), the editorial stated that the legal case against the Hindu temple management by the government was an unwise decision. It urged the government to withdraw the case unilaterally with immediate effect.

The journal lasted only a year. It merged with an Odia journal published from Balasore and came out under a new name called *Odia O Naba Sambad* in 1888; alternatively called *Jagannath Patrika*.

Odia O Naba Sambad (1888)

Published from Dey's Press, the journal had associates like Radhanath Ray, Madhusudan Rao, and Sadhu Charan Ray. It critiqued the anglicized youth that blindly aped the Western culture. Regretting the absence of quality textbooks in Odia in literature, the sciences, and maths, it spoke of the need to fill up this void at the earliest. It published several pieces of literary criticism of classical and modern texts. Literary essays related to Radhanath Ray published in various issues of the journal are particularly noteworthy. Radhanath's 'Self-condemnation of an Illustrious Man' was published on 21 August 1907 and a lengthy tribute to Bhudev Mukhopadhyay appeared on 23 May 1894.

Nationalistic poems and obituaries after the passing of Radhanath found place in the pages of the journal. Apart from these, it also published many news items such as the staging of Shakespeare's play *Macbeth* by the Ravenshaw College Students Association in 1897. It covered events from the national and international domains and successfully carried out its mission for over twenty-five years until the death of Baikunthanath Dey of Balasore in 1913.

Sambalpur Hitesini (1889)

The first periodical to come out from western Odisha was *Sambalpur Hitesini* (Nanda 2002). Edited by Nilamani Bidyaratna (1867–1924), *Hitesini* was brought out on 30 May 1889 by Bamanda's king, Sir Basudeva Sudhaladev (1850–1903). Speaking about the journal, *Utkal Dipika* dated 29 June 1889 wrote:

A new weekly called *Sambalpur Hitesini* has just started its publication. We gratefully acknowledge its receipt. The periodical does not mention the name of its printer or the press. However, since it is from Bamanda [Nanda 2008], it appears to be printed at the Jagannath Ballav Press. It comprises one demy-size paper and its annual subscription fee is two rupees. Thus it can be easily acquired compared to [the] other journals of Utkal. By its appearance, a great void has been filled up of Utkal which forms part of Madhya Pradesh. It will be a matter of pleasure for people here to take a look at this publication. We pray for its long life!

Indeed during the late nineteenth century, Bamanda was a confluence of many literary movements, both classical and modern. Writers like Bhubaneswar Badapanda, Madhusudan Mishra, Kali Charan Dwivedy, Brajabandhu Mishra, and others created a fertile literary ground in Bamanda whose king, Sudhaladev, established the Sudhala Press at Cuttack in 1885. Sudhaladev patronized two periodicals named *Sevaka* and *Samskaraka*.

Since some differences cropped up with regard to *Samskaraka*, Raja Sudhaladev shifted part of the press to Deogarh, which got merged with Jagannathballav Press in 1886. *Hitesini* functioned till 1923. Subsequently, Jagannathballav Press operated as Electric Machine Press till 1947, after which it has continued as the Government

Printing Press. While staying at Jobra, Cuttack, in 1872, Basudev Sudhaladev came in close contact with Gourishankar Ray, the editor of *Utkal Dipika*. He visited the Cuttack Printing Company and Mission Press, and decided to set up a press of his own.

Sudhaladev was reformatory in approach. He was keen to abolish superstition in the realm of religion, society, and culture, and eradicate child marriage, sati, and other evil practices. The journal initially appeared every Wednesday. Later, from 18 June 1904 onwards, it appeared every Saturday.

The editor of *Hitesini*, Nilamani Bidyaratna, was a distinguished man of letters, who also served as the editor of other periodicals like *Utkal Dipika* and *Prajabandhu* for a while. He played a pioneering role in the merger of the Odia-speaking areas, a movement that took the shape of an organization called Utkal Sammilani at a later period. As Mayadhar Mansingh wrote:

As the editor of *Prajabandhu* in the district of Ganjam then in Madras Presidency, Bidyaratna first organized a conference of the Odias in Madras in 1902 demanding unification of all Odia tracts. This gave birth to the larger Utkal Sammilani or the All Orissa Political Conference, which in its first session in 1903 brought to its platform Odias from all ranks and parts of the country demanding a homogenous Odia State. (1962: 213)

The range of the articles that Bidyaratna wrote was truly amazing. Public health, agriculture, untouchability, nature and natural life, and the place of libraries—nothing escaped the sharp gaze of Bidyaratna.

'Kali Bhagavata' appeared regularly in the first year of *Hitesini*. The column ridiculed the aberrations of the Brahmins and portrayed the class with a note of sarcasm. In the debate between the classical poet Upendra Bhanja and the modern Radhanath Ray, it preferred the latter. It defended Odia as the court language of the Sambalpur region vis-à-vis Hindi and published an article titled 'The Crisis of Language in Sambalpur'. Gangadhar Meher lamented the state of affairs in a poem entitled 'Bharata Rodan', published in *Sambalpur Hitesini* on 3 October 1894. Two other journals that appeared around this time were notable for the literary debates they carried out in their pages: *Indradhanu* (1893) from Cuttack and *Bijuli* (1893) from Bamanda.

Utkal Prabha (1891): Princely States

Patronized by the Maharaja of Mayurbhanj, Sri Ramachandra Bhanjadeo, *Utkal Prabha* began its publication from Baripada in April 1891. Hailed by the prominent writers of its time such as Fakir Mohan, this periodical became a powerful tool for the dissemination of news, views, translations, issued-based essays, criticism, and fiction. Printed from King's Press, Baripada, the journal, in the words of the maharaja, was meant to fill the void in the literary field: 'The educated sections of our nation do not evince an interest in writing essays and books due to a lack of interest and resources. To make up for this absence, there is a move to bring out a periodical from next month onwards. It will cover literature, science, philosophy, religion, and social conduct. It will reward outstanding writers' (*Mrutyunjaya Granthabali* 1971: 416). The subscription cost along with postage within Baripada was one-and-a-half rupees and outside Baripada it was two rupees per annum. It was reduced to one rupee from 1894 onwards.

Supported by the maharaja, the periodical appeared regularly for four years till 1896 and had three editors, Chaitanya Prasad Ray, Gobind Chandra Mohapatra, and Rajeswar Mohapatra respectively. The idea of recognizing well-deserving authors with prizes by *Utkal Prabha* generated its share of controversy in its pages as well as in other journals such as *Utkal Dipika*. Well-known author and correspondent Krishna Prasad Choudhury wrote to the maharaja regarding this matter and wished to know the reasons for the discontinuance of prizes. He suggested a replacement for the editor or the selection committee in case this was a necessity.[17] The move was opposed by others like Radhanath Ray who wrote to Gangadhar Meher regarding this issue.

Utkal Prabha's publication for the last issue of the first year gave details of the selection committee and the winners of the cash prizes as follows:

The awards committee comprised the following individuals of Baripada:

Sri Babu Mohini Mohan Dhar
Sri Gobinda Chandra Mohapatra Sharma,
Sri Babu Brundaban Chandra Panda[18]

The following were the recipients of prizes from the first to the sixth issue:

1. Khandagiri by Babu Chandra Mohan Maharana B.A.		Rs. 10/-
2. Mahabharata by Biswanath Kar		Rs. 10/-
3. Baidehi Bilapa 1st two Cantos by Babu Kanhailal Basu		Rs. 40/-
4. Basaba Bijaya 1st Canto		Rs. 10/-
5. Mo Sisu by Babu Gobinda Chandra Mahapatra Sharma		Rs. 20/-
6. Drushyaraji by Gobinda Chandra M. Sharma		Rs. 20/-
7. Himachala by Gobinda Chandra M. Sharma		Rs. 100/-
8. Chilika by Sri Babu Radhanath Ray		Rs. 100/-
Total		Rs. 310/-

Awards related to the seventh and eighth issue of *Utkal Prabha*:

1. Drusharaji by Sri Gobinda Chandra Mohapatra		Rs. 20/-
2. Sahitya Charcha by Sri Bijay Chandra Mazumdar		Rs. 15/-
3. Rishipane Debabatarana by Babu Madhusudan Rao		Rs. 50/-
4. Hitabadi Kie by Babu Ganapath Das B.A.		Rs. 15/-
5. Stree Sikhya by Sri Babu Biswanath Kar		Rs. 10/-
Total		Rs. 110/-

The periodical happened to get a bad name since many undeserving authors also got cash prizes. Prizes aside, the periodical played a significant role in publishing outstanding literary pieces including prose and poetry. Literary debates were also a prominent part of the journal, for instance, when Lala Ram Narayan wrote against the classicist Upendra Bhanja in favour of the modernist Radhanath, a respondent using a pseudonym called Hitabadi wondered if the so-called modern creativity was ever possible without a base of a literary tradition. 'Is Radhanath's poetry devoid of the Adi Rasas, the primary emotions?' it wondered. It felt amused to see the slavish habit of imitation of alien examples while neglecting worthy indigenous role models.[19] It is possible that this debate in *Utkal Prabha* later led to the publication of the literary journal *Indradhanu*.

Utkal Prabha published several outstanding works: 'The Civilizational History of the Aryas' by Chaitanya Prasad Ray; 'Parents and Offspring' by Parbati Charan Das; 'Freedom', 'Female Education', 'External Love', and other pieces by Biswanath Kar. The journal also gave prominence to modern writers like Radhanath Ray, Gangadhar Meher, Madhusudan Rao, and Fakir Mohan Senapati. Ram Shankar Ray's historical novel *Bibasini* also appeared serially in this journal in the context where novel reading was considered in many quarters as an immoral act.

Next in line among the eminent literary periodicals was *Utkal Sahitya* (1897), which, along with *Utkal Dipika* (1866), will be taken up separately for discussion. It would be useful to look at the role of some other periodicals which made a difference to the literary–cultural life of the pre-Independence and post-Independence Odisha. The first decade of the twentieth century witnessed the advent of the literary magazine called *Satyabadi*, which served as a manifesto for the writers and reformers associated with the Satyabadi School.

Edited by Pandit Gopabandhu Das, *Satyabadi* was first published in February–March of 1915. Its masthead proclaimed the pursuit of truth as its main goal. Printed by Asha Press of Brahmapur, it devoted columns and pages to the discussion of regional and foreign literatures, education, especially the system of national education, and original articles on politics, philosophy, and history.

Gopabandhu underlined the importance of literature for the masses. Literature that is acceptable to the common folks, he terms as 'Loukika Sahitya'. He wrote:

By denying literature to the commoners, national literature can never be produced. It is no one's claim that literature should not assume higher forms in terms of thought, emotions, and idioms, but it must be expressed in a simple and lucid manner to become part of the national wealth. In other words, national literature has to embody national life and the national spirit.[20]

He regretted the neglect of the Odia language and the literary traditions by the ruling elites in Odisha and championed the cause of the mother tongue. Above all, he laid the greatest emphasis on the development of critical temper through a systematic use of literary criticism. There was a separate section devoted to students, called 'Chhatra Bhaga'. Contributed to mostly by Gopabandhu himself, this section made the students aware of higher thoughts, ethical conduct, and the national spirit. Speaking of the importance of *bana bidyalaya* or forest schools, he felt that it was much better and far economical to impart education beneath the trees than to spend a huge amount of money on the construction of schools. He gave the utmost importance to universal education.[21] Further, education through the mother tongue would narrow the gap between the educated and uneducated classes. Regardless of the advanced planning of the modern university and political–administrative system, it was only the mother-tongue education that could create harmony among the different sections of the people and bring them together.

Like mother-tongue education, rural development was another important goal of *Satyabadi* which created a separate section called 'Palliprasanga' to discuss the problems related to village life. Gopabandhu wrote:

There are many noble souls in the villages. They are God fearing and do not wish ill of others. They face hardship for themselves and yet seek others' welfare and that of the whole village. Such people are there in every village, but who recognizes them and who encourages them? There are many Gokhales, Vidyasagars, and Pyari Mohans among them, but who is keeping an account of such people? Neglected by others and denied of any help and encouragement, they are destined to bloom and wither unseen like the forest flowers. No one understands the fact that such people constitute the real strength of a nation.[22]

Gopabandhu gave a clarion call for self-reliance and self-rule of the villages. Indeed he believed that in the welfare of the villages lies the well-being of the nation. In his writings, he aptly chose the village as the scene of action. *Satyabadi* excelled in publishing historical essays as well. Gopabandhu believed that by the reading of history and earlier chronicles, one gathers strength and becomes self-reliant.[23]

Krupasindhu Mishra, a teacher in the Satyabadi School, established a history club and held discussions on historical themes. He published many essays such as the 'Spread of the British Empire in India', 'Hindu Social System', etc. Similarly, Birupaksha Kar wrote serially on the Kesari dynasty. Jagabandhu Singh too wrote on historical themes. Gopabandhu and Pandit Nilakantha Das wrote on social problems. Pandit Nilakantha wrote on science for the masses and the base of nationalism, just as others such as Basudev Mohapatra, Lingaraj Mishra, Ratnakar Pati, and Godabarish Mishra published insightful essays on a variety of topics of contemporary relevance. In order to maintain its solemnity, *Satyabadi* refrained from publishing poetry, short story, and fiction.[24]

Satyabadi was published regularly for six years. After Gopabandhu started the daily *Samaja* on 4 October 1919 and was greatly preoccupied in the new venture, *Satyabadi* lost its periodicity. Later, Pandit Nilakantha Das published a journal called *Naba Bharata* that was patterned after *Satyabadi*.

During its existence, *Satyabadi* functioned as a major instrument for nationalistic thought and action. It brought together the message of the region, the nation, and the world under one umbrella. It preached the all-important message of village self-governance as a necessary requisite to national reconstruction.[25]

Sahakar (1919): Path Towards Socialism

This socialistic periodical first appeared in 1919 from Puri under the leadership of Lakshminarayan Sahu. After ten years, Balakrishna Kar took charge of this periodical that published prose, poetry, fiction, comic verse, popular science, and related matter. It gave special importance to the publication of novels in serialized form under the series called 'Ananada Lahari Upanyasamal'. They comprised Kalindi Charan's *Matira Manisha* (The Son of the Soil), Chintamani Mishra's *Hatha Bhagya* (The Unfortunate One), Godabarish Mohapatra's

Prema Pathe (In the Path of Love), Harischandra Badal's *Chhithira Jabab* (The Reply of the Letter), and Kanhu Charan Mohanty's *Nishpath* (The Decision).

Similarly, women writers like Sarala Devi wrote on 'Gana Sahitya' and Kuntala Kumari Sabat wrote 'Delhi Chithi' (Letter from Delhi). The latter focused attention on the various sessions of the Indian National Congress, integration of the princely states, and plight of the Odias in the outlying areas.

Likewise, many poets such as Mayadhar Mansingh, Kalindi Charan Panigrahi, and Guru Prasad Mohanty published their early work in *Sahakar*. It appeared regularly till 1952. It was briefly edited by Kalindi Charan. From 1973 onwards, it was edited by Bichitrananda Kar and later by Pathani Patnaik. However, it must be admitted that the later incarnations do not have the same standard as the original ones.

Naba Bharata (1934): Pandit Nilakantha Das

As a daily and monthly, *Naba Bharata* remains an important milestone in the history of Odia periodicals. In 1933, after being released from jail, Pandit Nilakantha wished to start a new periodical with 5,000 rupees that he received from the Maharaja of Jeypore, Bikram Dev. With this money as an 'endowment', he bought a press from Pandit Ganeshwar Mishra of Dhenkanal and *Naba Bharata* appeared in June 1934.

The new journal received negative treatment in the hands of Biswanath Kar who treated *Naba Bharata* as an infant and considered its editor essentially an egocentric individual. He urged the editor to be free from mannerism and devote himself to the real pursuit of literature.[26] It is possible that underlying Kar's trenchant criticism was perhaps a degree of professional rivalry. Undeterred, the periodical appeared regularly from June 1934 to 1942 and again from October 1946 to March 1955.

In the first issue of the first year, *Naba Bharata* published the work of Mayadhar Mansingh, Lakhmidhara Nayak, Bimbadhar Barma, Girija Shankar Ray, Godabarish Mishra, Harapriya Dei, Shashi Bhushan Ray, and Sita Devi Khadenga in the domain of prose and poetry.

Editing was Nilakantha's forte and he paid attention to details even as he was discerning about the selection of contributions. The journal promoted a fresh approach in literature and brought in perspectives from the national and international levels. Another unique feature was the manner in which the editorials were taken up for discussion. The editorial on Utkal Sahitya Samaj in *Naba Bharata*, seventy year, volume I, number 4 serves as an appropriate example:

The main reason for the poverty of Odisha is the poverty of its literature. Just as national literature grows along with the growth of the individual character, in the same manner, the development of the national character would also lead to the blossoming of the individual self. Unfortunately, nothing seems to be happening in Odisha.

The big Pandits do not discuss literature and those that discuss literature do not desire to be Pandits....

It is essential to rescue Odia literature from such a beaten path. The direction will be shown by the Professors of Odisha. We must soon gather plenty of books in Cuttack. Along with, we need to kindle an interest in book reading and undertake scientific discussions among the youth of today. Two institutions can carry this out: The Ravenshaw College and the Utkal Sahitya Samaj. Elsewhere, to a limited extent exist Parala Khemundi, Baripada, and Mayurbhanj.

Similarly, in discussing the internal politics of the Congress Party, Nilakantha suggested that the rebellion within the party ought to be harnessed for constructive purposes. He wrote, 'It is not desirable that leaders like Subhas Chandra Bose and Manabendra Nath Roy are today outside the party.'[27] The editorials reveal Nilakantha as fiercely independent and creative in his approach.

A newspaper called *Naba Bharata* was born in November 1941 under the editorship of Nilakantha Das. As the editor of the paper, Das never compromised with high standards. As a result, after five years of publication, the paper closed down in October 1946. During their lifetimes, both the periodical and the newspaper showed Nilakantha as an outstanding journalist and litterateur who combined tradition and modernity with effortless ease.

Adhunika (1935): **Progressive Movement in Odisha**

Carrying only six volumes, *Adhunika* became the mouthpiece of the progressive literary movement in Odisha. It was the main organ of the Nabajuga Sahitya Samsad which was formed in 1935 and whose main sessions were held from 29 November 1935 to 4 December 1935. Supported by Nilakantha Das, an announcement was made regarding the new publication in the pages of *Naba Bharata*. Edited by the Marxist author Bhagabati Charan Panigrahi, the periodical desired to promote the various literary genres that would enthuse the 'place and spirit of work' and relate to the various social movements. Abjuring the Odia Romanticism, several writers like Ananta Patnaik, Gurucharan Patnaik, Pranabandhu Kar, Gopinath Mohanty, and Sachi Routray wrote in the social–realistic mode, both prose and poetry. Much of the literature was composed in the Marxist mould. It spoke against the tyranny of different kinds and upheld socialistic resistance. Ananta Patnaik wrote against Romanticism as a form of escapism, just as Bhagabati Charan hailed the formation of the International Federation of Writers, which believed in equality and a classless society. After Bhagabati Charan's passing, there was an attempt in November 1974 by Ramnath Panda to revive this journal, but it did not last long. Although confined to six years, *Adhunika* made a place for itself in the Odia periodical literature.

Shankha

Patronized by the Maharaja of Bamanda, this periodical was edited by Mayadhar Mansingh and later, for a while, by Jalandhar Dev. The journal became a major forum for discussion of the Odia Romantic literature. Krishna Chandra Panigrahi's essay 'Sabuja Saili' (The Romantic Idiom) can be considered a major contribution to the understanding of Odia Romanticism. The journal brought the folk poet Baishnab Pani into the limelight and underlined the importance of essays on grammar written by Bamadev Mishra and Bidhubhushan Guru. The editorials by Mansingh in *Shankha* were particularly noteworthy. He wrote fearlessly and spoke against corruption in the domains of literature and education. In due course, the journal became a victim of its outspokenness.

Chaturanga (1946)

Like *Shankha*, its counterpart *Chaturanga* was first published from Balangir on 14 May 1946. It was preceded in terms of publication by *Ralinga* (1932), *Patna Gazette* (1935), and *Patna Dipika* (1941). Patronized by Maharaja Rajendra Narayan Singh Deo, the journal was edited by Brajendra Narayan Singh Deo. A cultural organization called Kosala Kalamandal was begun as the main support base of the journal. It comprised writers like Kalindi Charan Panigrahi, Balavadra Bahidhar, Prabhat Kumar Mukhopadhyaya, Nityananda Bahidar, Bidhubhushan Guru, and Samuel Nayak.

The main aim of this journal was to undertake discussions related to literature, dance, music, and the fine arts. Like *Shankha*, *Chaturanga* too paid its contributors five rupees per piece. Its main authors were Raj Kishore Ray, Gouri Kumar Brahma, Kanhu Charan Mishra, Lakshmi Narayan Mohanty, Pranabandhu Kar, Surendra Mohanty, Gopinath Mohanty, and Nityananda Mohapatra.

Similarly, its leading poets comprised Baikuntanath Patnaik, Kalindi Charan Panigrahi, Sachi Routray, Mayadhar Mansingh, Binod Nayak, Chintamani Behera, and Benudhar Rout. The periodical lasted till 1951. Short-lived, *Chaturanga* will remain a milestone due to the remarkable manner in which it was brought out from a relatively inaccessible Balangir and dealt with literature, music, dance, and the fine arts.

Jhankar (1949)

Initially published as the Sunday literary page of the daily *Prajatantra*, *Jhankar* the periodical was born in April 1949. In the third year of its publication, the editorial of *Jhankar* stated that the journal appeared without much preparation. It was meant to supplement the efforts of

Prajatantra in order to give a new direction to Odia literature. In order to carry out this task, the chief editor, Harekrushna Mahatab, constituted an editorial board comprising the following members: Mayadhar Mansingh, Sadashiv Mishra, Kalindi Charan Panigrahi, and Janaki Ballav Patnaik.

At different times, the journal was managed by a host of literary luminaries like Chakradhar Samal, Pathani Patnaik, Mohapatra Nilamani Sahu, and others. It is currently edited by Saroj Ranjan Mohanty. The opening edition of the journal carried pieces on topics such as modern poetry, the Natha community of Utkal, determining the date of the *Rig Veda*'s composition, the Gandhian man and his life, the wealth of Chilika, literature and its tradition, disease and its remedy, and so on. The contributors were eminent men and women of letters such as Raj Kishore Ray, Bidyut Prabha Devi, Gouri Kumar Brahma, Gagan Bihara Mohanty and Manoj Das. Accompanied by Bishuba Milan, a gathering of poets and authors, *Jhankar* has carved out a space for itself in the literary–cultural life of Odisha. The journal gave primacy in the later years to original and experimental writings. The best of the modern poetry of Sachi Routray, Guruprasad Mohanty, Ramakant Rath, Sitakant Mohapatra, Soubhagya Kumar Mishra, and Rajendra Kishore Panda has appeared in its pages. Similarly, it has also published research-based articles by critics like Krishna Chandra Panigrahi, Bansidhar Mohanty, Natabar Samantaray, Srinibas Mishra, Dasarath Das, Nityananda Satpathy, and others. There have been publications of essays on the Odia language and script by critics like Golak Biharu Dhal, Kunja Bihari Tripathy just as Astaballar Mohanty, Nilakantha Das, Jaykrishna Mishra, Gangadhar Bal, and others have written on philosophy and literary criticism in the pages of *Jhankar*. The journal has given space to a variety of genres including prose, poetry, travelogues, drama, short story, and literary criticism. It may, therefore, be safely said that many of the most established writers of contemporary Odisha began their career from the pages of *Jhankar*.

Asanta Kali (1950)

A monthly that was published from Calcutta since 1950, *Asanta Kali* was managed at different times by writers like Hrudananda Mallick, Jadumani Paruja, Srikanta Panda, Shyam Sundar Mohapatra, Kanduri Charan Das, and Kali Charan Das. The contributions in the periodical aimed at a popular audience rather than a highbrow one. Its authors included some of the best known in Odisha such as Sachi Routray, Radha Mohan Gadnaik, Surendra Mohanty, Gopinath Mohanty and Ramakanta Rath. It had a separate section for women, children, and youth and published prose, poetry, and fiction on a regular basis.

Konarka (1958)

The mouthpiece of the Odisha Sahitya Akademi, *Konarka* came out as a tri-quarterly from 1958 onwards. It gives space to prose, poetry, and fiction and has brought out special issues on different occasions. It attempts to realize the main goals of the Sahitya Akademi in literary terms and concentrates on the classical and modern Odia literature, comparative approach to the Odia culture, exploring the underlying unity of Indian literatures as well as the relationship between Odia literature and allied art forms such as dance, drama, music, architecture, and sculpture.

In the initial issues, the journal devoted its pages to the classical literatures and thought of India, such as the *Rig Veda*, *Dandi Ramayana* and the Buddhist tradition in Odisha, the linguistic heritage of Odisha, the nation and literature, spirituality in the Indian dance traditions, and so on. Similarly, the journal has brought out special issues on 'Pancha Sakhas', Fakir Mohan and Upendra Bhanja, as well as on specific genres like the short story, poetry, and essays. Clearly, the dream of its first editor, Gouri Kumar Brahma, has not been realized, but the periodical at present maintains its regularity and acts as an effective mouthpiece of the Sahitya Akademi.

Pourusa (1967)

Established and edited by Janaki Ballav Patnaik and Jayanti Patnaik in 1967, the journal gives primacy to essays dealing with religion, philosophy, and spirituality. Its main aim is to make popular the writings of spiritual figures like Gandhi, Sri Ramakrishna, Swami Vivekananda, and Sri Aurobindo. It has published stories from India and abroad and translations and adaptations from K.M. Munshi's *Krishna Avatars*, Bankim Chandra's *Bisha Brukhya*, and Vyasa's Mahabharata.

Naba Rabi (1970)

Now extinct, this journal appeared in July 1970 and was published from Calcutta. Its publisher and patron was Rabindra Kumar Parija and it was managed by Bibhuti Patnaik and Kanduri Charan Das. In its first editorial, the journal promised to reach out to every nook and corner of Odisha, and to be taken to every connoisseur of Odia literature. It attracted some of the best and most eminent writers from Odisha such as Kalindi Charan Panigrahi, Rabindranath Singh, Sachi Routray, Radha Mohan Gadnayak, Manoj Das, Santanu Acharya, Sitakant Mohapatra, Ramakanta Rath, Kanhu Charan Mohanty, and Gopinath Mohanty. The journal attempted a mix of the older and younger authors and brought together both tradition and modernity.

Manas (1972)

Published for the first time in 1972, the journal *Manas* became known as an intellectual forum that was illustrated and that reached out to the intelligentsia. It discussed the literary issues of the day and brought under its ambit writers and essayists like Bidhubhushan Das, Krushna Prasad Mishra, Mohapatra Nilamani Sahu, Yashodhara Mishra, Srinivas Udgata, Souri Bandhu Kar, Ganeshwara Mishra, Suryakanta Das, Chandra Sekhar Rath, and Sitakant Mahapatra. Edited by Krushna Prasad Mishra, the journal was established by Ananta Mishra. The illustrations were by the well-known artist Asit

Mukherjee and added to the overall effect of the magazine. It ceased publication from March 1981.

Apart from these, several periodicals and magazines appeared in the twentieth century. They included *Adhuna* (1973), *Istahar* (1975), *Eshana* (1980), *Kumkum* (1948), *Katha* (1987), *Galpa* (1970), *Galpa Jhara* (1977), *Gokarnika* (1982), *Chandrika* (1953), *Dagara* (1936), *Diganta* (1950), *Naba Patra* ((1962), *Pragyan* (1960), *Pancha Ranga* (1970), *Baruni* (1975), *Baisi Pahacha* (1976), *Basundhara* (1981), *Mulyayana* (1979), *Juga Bina* (1933), *Samabesa*, *Sanjoga*, and *Naba Lipi*.

A Rich Social History

Many of the journals discussed above are now extinct. However, during their existence some of them made a difference to the literary–cultural life of Odisha. Clearly, they are no match for their counterparts in the late nineteenth and early twentieth centuries. Perhaps the colonial period generated a literary–cultural crisis that has not been witnessed in the post-Independence period.

The periodical press in colonial Odisha, for the most part, was not subversive or seditious in nature, and therefore it received support from the government. Both John Beames and T.E. Ravenshaw were lovers of the Odia language and literature. The press pointed out administrative flaws and defended press freedom vis-à-vis the Licensing Press Act of 1878, just as *Utkal Sahitya* cried out against the purchase of foreign goods.[28] This led the commissioner of the Odisha division to state that the Odia people, peace-loving by nature, were kept away from politics and were interested mainly in the resolution of local problems.

Constraints

Out of the 26 journals that had initially appeared in Odisha during 1880, by 1881 only six were active in the field. Circulation was limited and subscription, as the novelist Fakir Mohan stated, was in many cases nominal. He wrote in *Balasore Sambad Bahika*: 'The number of nominal subscribers ranged from forty and fifty, but the price was actually collected from eight or ten. The number of persons who read it ranged between twenty and twenty-five' (Behera and Dash 2000: 51). *Utkal Sahitya* wrote with deep regret: 'It is universally acknowledged that the journals are the best means of developing a language. But why is there so much of distaste for them in Orissa.'[29] Several factors were responsible for the state of affairs. Mrutyunjay Rath identified five: (a) improper management, (b) lack of resources, (c) editors' lack of qualification and skill, (d) relative absence of competent contributors, and (e) insufficient number of subscribers (*Mrutyunjaya Granthabali* 1971: 421).

Achievements

Despite the constraints, the press in Odisha led to the advent of modern prose and poetry; the printing of classical writing led to the development of a comparative approach to the study of the classical and modern literatures. Social reforms, female education and the anti-caste movement were all propelled by the press during the nineteenth century in Odisha.

———

The extract from the journal *Pradipa*, cited as the epigraph to this chapter, shows the centrality of the periodical press in shaping the colonial/alternative project in Odisha. By the 1930s, attention of the press had shifted to the need for political unification of the Odia-speaking people, taking the colonial modernity project to the larger domain. In the next chapter, we shall look closely at two of the leading journals of the period, their genesis, and the way their founders, Gourishankar Ray and Biswanath Kar, contributed to the making of the new Odia imaginary.

Notes

1. All translations from Odia into English used in the chapter, unless otherwise indicated, are by me.

2. I am indebted to Bauribandhu Kar for the valuable information regarding Odia periodical literature. See also Mishra (1979 [1983]), Pattanayak (1972), Pradhan (1973, 1995), and Samantaray (1964).

3. See also William Bolts, 'A Short Chronological Narrative of Events [1801]', Cleveland Public Library, John G. White Zamboni ms Wq 091.92, B 639s, f. 4.

4. Hickey is rightly regarded as the father of Indian journalism, and his role is remembered till today by his admirers as would be noticed from the following news report, date marked Agra, 2 February 2011, entitled 'Agra Scribes Remember James Augustus Hickey, India's First Journalist': 'Speaking on the occasion, veteran journalist Neville Smith said: "Free press in India owes a debt of gratitude to James Augustus Hickey, the man who almost single-handedly faced the might of the British empire in India to espouse the cause of free expression and reining in of the government by the voice of the people, exposing the actions of the government, and making public the dirty deals."'

Considered a highly eccentric Irishman, he founded the country's first newspaper called *Hickey's Bengal Gazette* or the *Calcutta General Advertiser* and allowed it 'to become the channel of personal invective, and the most scurrilous abuse of individuals of all ranks, high and low, rich and poor, many were attacked in the most wanton and cruel manner'. See http:/www.agratoday.in/news/index

5. The collection comprises two components essentially, along with the years of publications available: firstly, newspapers that were once part of the British Museum library, and secondly, newspaper-holdings from the former India Office library. The collection includes the following: *Hickey's Bengal Gazette* (1780–1782), the *Hircarrah* (1794), the *Bengal Catholic Expositor* and the *Bengal Hurkaru*, the *Bombay Courier*, the *Bombay Gazette* (1792–1868), the *Asiatic Mirror, and Commercial Advertiser* (1798), the *Catholic Herald* (1841), the *Bengal Herald* (1843), *Bengal Lottery* (1793), *Bengal Weekly Messenger* (1825), *Bombay Times* (1841), *Calcutta Courier and Civil, Military and Naval Gazette* (1840–1842), *Calcutta Literary Gazette* (1832), the *Calcutta Morning Post* (1812–1813) *Calcutta Morning Post Extraordinary* (1793), *East India Political Register* (1838–1839), the *Friend of India* (1820–1835), the *Friend of India and Statesman* (1877–1883), *Government Gazette* (1815–1832), the *Half Weekly Calcutta Courier* (1839), the *Madras Courier* (1790–1791), the *Madras Gazette* (1795–1799), *Madras Herald*

(1841–1842), *Madras Mail Asylum Herald* (1833–1836), the *Madras Native Herald* (1845), the *Military Gazette* (1834), the *Oriental Commercial Register and East India Press* (1818–1819), *Oriental Observer* (1828–1831), *Oriental Observer and Literary Chronicle* (1837–1839), the *Oriental Star* (1793), *Overland Courier* (1840–1841), *Summary of Indian Intelligence* (1839–1853), the *Times* (1813), the *United Service Gazette* (1839), *United Service Gazette and Literary Chronicle* (1841–1842), the *Weekly Examiner* (1840–1841), the *Weekly Intelligencer* (1841) and the *World* (1794). See the nineteenth-century British Library newspapers database on http:/www.bl.uk/reshelp/findhel-prestype/news (accessed on 3 July 2015).

6. Banshidhar Mohanty's volume is an excellent compilation of *Utkal Dipika* of 1866. It has a very useful and informative 'Introduction'.

7. Nihar Ranjan Patnaik, 'Missionaries and their Social Impact on 19th Century Orissa', *The Orissa History Research Journal (OHRJ)*, XXXV (1 and 2); Dasarathi Suara, 'The Christian Missionary Activities in Orissa and their Impact on 19th Century', *The Orissa History Research Journal (OHRJ)*, XXXIV (1 and 2).

8. For a comprehensive account of the role of the missionaries in Odisha, see Dhall (1997).

9. *Utkal Dipika*, 24 August 1867, p. 134.

10. Part 1 (1869) and Part 2 (1870). Quoted in the 'Introduction' to Behera and Dash (2000), pp. 3, 9.

11. *Utkal Dipika*, 26 January 1878, p. 14.

12. *Utkal Dipika*, 26 January 1878, p. 15.

13. *Utkal Dipika*, 2 February 1878, p. 20.

14. *Utkal Dipika*, 20/5, 31 January 1885, p. 34.

15. *Utkal Dipika*, 20/9, 28 February 1885, p. 76.

16. *Naba Sambad*, 31 March 1887, p. 39.

17. *Utkal Dipika*, 29/23, 9 June 1894, pp. 180–1.

18. *Utkal Prabha*, 1/12, 1891, p. 327.

19. *Utkal Dipika*, 27/22, 28 May 1892, pp. 173–4.

20. *Satyabadi*, Vol. 3, Parts 3 and 4, p. 73.

21. *Satyabadi*, Vol. 1, Parts 10 and 11, p. 303.

22. *Satyabadi*, Vol. 1, No. 4, p. 107.

23. *Satyabadi*, Vol. 1, No. 12, p. 355.

24. *Satyabadi*, Vol. 1, Nos 1 and 2, p. 5.

25. *Satyabadi*, Vol. 2, Nos 1 and 2, p. 5.

26. *Utkal Sahitya*, Vol. 38, No. 3, p. 113.

27. *Naba Bharata*, Seventh year, No. 1.

28. Annual General Administrative Report, Orissa Division, 1891–2. p. 27.

29. *Utkal Sahitya*, Baisakha, 1304, p. 90.

2

The Editors: Gourishankar Ray
and Biswanath Kar

Despite changes in historiography, biographical approaches to the study of social and cultural phenomena have not become dated. While older versions of leadership studies have been given up, newer approaches such as dealing with individual agency in print capitalism have found merit. It is from this vantage point that we shall look at the life and times of the two editors Gourishankar Ray and Biswanath Kar in this chapter.

A biographer of the two editors faces considerable difficulty: Most accounts available in the public domain in Odisha are scanty in nature and are repetitive; few biographies are critical in approach. Most are celebratory, given the cult stature both the editors enjoy in the state. My intention here is to acquaint the readers with a modicum of facts about the two editors while closer attention will be paid to the contents and ideology of the two journals in the next two chapters.

Gourishankar Ray

Most biographers of Gourishankar agree that his ancestors came from Bengal and got domiciled in Odisha, as the region was known then. It is believed that they arrived in their adopted land during the revenue administration of Todar Mal, Emperor Akbar's revenue minister. Initially carrying the title 'Boshus', in due course they assumed the surname 'Ray' (Rath 1997).[1] Gourishankar's grandfather, Madhab Prasad, a Vaishnavite, looked after the Sakhi Math of Puri. He had four sons, the eldest of whom, Sadashiv Prasad, fathered four children. Gourishankar was the eldest and Ramashankar the youngest of the four (Rath 1997: 2).

Family Life

Gourishankar was born on 13 July 1838 in Dikhitpada in the erstwhile Cuttack district, around the time Bankim Chandra Chatterjee took birth in the Kanthalpara village in Bengal. After receiving early education in the village *pathashala* (school), at the age of eleven, Gourishankar went to read Odia, Urdu, and Persian in the high school at Cuttack in 1849. In 1858, universities were set up in Calcutta, Bombay, and Madras. Gourishankar excelled in studies and winning a scholarship in 1856, he travelled to Hooghly in June 1857 for higher education. The task was far from easy. Apart from the distance, there was also the societal bias then against English education, which was alleged to have a 'corrupting' influence on young learners.

Gourishankar fared well in the first year at the Hooghly College but had to abandon his studies soon after, due to the bidding of his father in November 1858. On his way back, he worked as a temporary teacher at the Balasore Zilla School for 20 rupees per month, and subsequently returned to Cuttack in 1859 (Rath 1989: 3). Joining as a clerk at the commissioner's office, Cuttack, for 50 rupees in the latter half of 1859 (Ray 1989: 26), he was soon appointed as a money order agent by the then commissioner, G.F. Cockburn. He obtained a position as a translator. Fearless and independent-minded, Gourishankar was dutiful to a fault and stood up to his superior, Armstrong, the joint magistrate.

Independence of Mind

As Radhanath Rath records a memorable event:

In course of his work as a Money Order Clerk, one day the Joint Magistrate, Mr Armstrong, asked Gourishankar to accept a money order at late hours of the day ... Gourishankar politely refused as the scheduled time for accepting money order was over, saying would he deviate from the rules in favor of a superior officer, he might face an embarrassing situation when he would refuse to accept money orders from the public beyond time. He wanted to follow strictly the rules. When it was reported to the Joint Magistrate, Mr Armstrong, that Gourishankar had refused to accept the money order on the ground that the scheduled time was over, he got angry and personally came down to Gourishankar, when the latter was about to close his office and go. Gourishankar politely refused and said: 'I should make no discrimination between my Magistrate and a common man.' (Ray 1989: 3–4)

When the magistrate reported this matter to the commissioner, Gourishankar emphatically stated that 'a public servant makes no discrimination between a magistrate in authority and a common man, who are equal in eyes of rule and law' (Ray 1989). The commissioner's decision was in favour of Gourishankar and the magistrate was transferred. Thus, Gourishankar distinguished himself by devotion to service. Displaying exemplary honesty, he retired from government service in 1882 after a productive career.

Language Politics

Gourishankar was deeply concerned about the need to preserve the Odia language against the onslaught of Bengali. In 1868, Rajendralal Mitra, an administrator, addressed the Cuttack Debating Society and declared that those who believed in the welfare of the Odias ought to introduce Bengali as the lingua franca in the Odia-speaking areas, a viewpoint that was strongly supported by Umacharan Haldar and Rajakrishna Bandopadhyaya in *Cuttack Star*. After all, opined Mitra: 'Should there be a language for a population of 2,000,000 only?'[2] Further, Kanti Chandra Bhattacharya, a school teacher of Balasore, argued that 'Odia is not a separate language', but merely a dialect of Bengali.

Undeterred by Umacharan Haldar, Gourishankar satirically commented in *Utkal Dipika*:

The Baboo must be considered a well wisher of Orissa as he has invested a lot of time and energy for the spread of Oriya among the non-Oriyas to which his writings stand a witness. He has presented very strong reasons in favor of his arguments. The main argument is that Oriya scripts are written with the pen, ink and on paper of Bengal, why shouldn't we then adopt the Bengali script? If [the] people of this land have any knowledge on these three items, let them remember that they (these articles) were first discovered in Bengal and the origin of the words such as 'Kalam' (pen), 'Sihai' (ink) and 'kagaj' (paper) definitely suggests the same to prove the Baboo's intelligence and knowledge of facts. The Baboo not only presented this clever argument but also a subsequent one which is still a strange fact. The Baboo carefully compared the Oriya script with that of the Bengali ones and found the latter to be more beautiful and charming. Everyone loves his own child. The Oriya scripts are round in shape while the Bengali are triangular or half round ones. The latter scripts perhaps appeared to be attired in jewelry and gems or the 'Tribhanga' style of Lord Krishna got embodied in them which filled up the heart of the Baboo with deep Vaishnavite thoughts and devotion.[3]

The best way to preserve the Odia language, Gourishankar reasoned, would be through the medium of printing. A group of like-minded activists including Babu Bichitrananda Das, Jagmohan Ray, Maharaja Bhagirath Mahendra Bahadur of Dhenkanal, and Gourishankar Ray came together and established the Cuttack Printing Company with a capital investment of 7,500 rupees. Set up in the drawing room of Jagmohan Ray, the improvised litho press was operated by Bhagirathi Sathia.[4]

Realizing the absence of good textbooks in Odia, Gourishankar wrote a geography book and got it printed in his press along with many ancient texts transcribed from their palm-leaf origins. The main objective of the printing press was to bring out a weekly for the dissemination of news. Accordingly, a month after the establishment of the press, in August 1865, the first issue of *Utkal Dipika* was published. The appearance of the journal could not have been more timely, for in 1866 Odisha was devastated by a horrific famine called Na-anka Durbhikha. The Famine Enquiry Commission set up by the government of India under the chairmanship of George Campbell stated, among other things, the following:

The incident of mortality never will be ascertained with accuracy. Mr Ravenshaw, in his report of November first, estimates it not less than one fourth of the population of the province. In the supplementary report of November 6th, he shows that in the subdivision of Kendrapara alone, one fourth of the people are estimated to have died before 1st August, and the mortality consequent to that date, and having been part of the country alluded to, very considerably aggravated by flood, indicates a more excessive proportion in particular parts. (Rath 1997: 7)

The report captured the essential pathos of the situation:

The famine in Orissa stands almost alone in this, that there was (till a comparatively late period in history) almost no importation and the people shut up in a narrow province between pathless jungle and unnavigable sea, were in the condition of passengers in a ship without provision. Things came to such a pass that money was spurned as worthless; prices were constantly merely nominal, the rates are far beyond than known in any famine in this century of which we have known. (Rath 1997: 7)

It goes to the credit of the British that they took up this issue for discussion in the British parliament. Horrified by the nature of this tragedy, Sir Stafford Northcote remarked on the floor of the House of Commons: 'I feel for the unnaturalness of territorial dismemberment and suggest to bring the Oriya country under one separate administration. The whole province is geographically isolated to an excess degree … The people are also separate and distinct of a character and a language peculiar to themselves' (Rath 1997: 17).

Sir Stafford's considered opinion regarding the need for a more lasting solution to the tragedies of Odisha seems to have been echoed by Gourishankar himself in the Minutes of Evidence he gave to the Famine Commission dated 11 January 1867. I quote an extract from the Evidence:

I believe the most important of remedial measures would be a permanent settlement of the land revenue. If the demand of [the] Government were fixed, the land-holders would take greater interest on their estates and would try to improve them, so that the produce would be increased. I consider that a temporary settlement is injurious, because for some years before its close, they allow their estates to deteriorate, so that no increased assessment may be imposed on them at the resettlement. I believe that this has been done lately in Orissa. The country is now improving rapidly, and I believe that, if a permanent settlement were now made, the sons and grandsons of the present zamindars would be more liberal-minded than they are, and would really improve their estates. I do not consider that the zamindars or rajahs, who hold the killahas or estates, which are permanently settled, and which pay very little revenue, have brought their estates into better condition than the zamindars of the Mugalbundi or temporarily settled estates. I believe this is owing to the fact that the rajahs are a different and less advanced class of men. The Rajah of Dhenkanal is, however, an exception, and has much improved his killahas. I do not believe that the zamindars are exerting their influence to prevent their ryots from taking the Irrigation Company's water. I believe that the sole cause of the ryots holding back is the high price which is demanded, and the fact that they have no experience of the advantages which will ensue from irrigation.

I believe that if a permanent settlement were concluded, the zamindars would use their influence to induce the ryots to take the water. (Das et al. 1989: 75–6)

Famine Narratives

As the editor of *Utkal Dipika*, Gourishankar covered the news of the famine extensively and brought to public attention and to the notice of government officials, public grievances regarding income tax, salt tax, and sales tax apart from the issues of misgovernance by the police, civic,

and educational officials. Such action required a great deal of courage, for the press was bound to attract punitive action by vindictive officials for the forthrightness of the views expressed. Gourishankar's uniqueness lay in the fact that he presented all issues in an objective and dispassionate manner before its readership. He was present at the Royal Asiatic Society along with other Odia pundits and patriots at Calcutta in 1870 and vehemently opposed the imposition of Bengali as a court language in Orissa (Rath 1989: 9).

The campaigns he actively led in the pages of *Dipika* covered many issues such as the government's decision to withdraw Persian from the court, the need for the preservation of the Odia language and literature in Odisha as well as the preparation of standard textbooks. He wrote an effective rejoinder to Rajendralal Mitra's speech in *Dipika* and declared trenchantly that 'the ignorant ought not to pass a comment on a matter [on] which he had no knowledge'. His words are worth quoting here:

We thought that Rajendra Baboo had acquired a lot of knowledge on Orissa. But we are thunderstruck having heard such views expressed by him. It is difficult to say whether he expressed his own views or he had been influenced by exterior forces to pass such comments in favor of his mother tongue Bengali. Doesn't he know that the population figure he quotes is related only to the Mugalbundi area? The Oriya speaking areas extend from Medinipur in the North to Ganjam in the South and from the Bay of Bengal in the East to Sambalpur in the West. When he doesn't know this simple truth, why did he offer a chance to the audience to share his ignorance? And by doing so, doesn't he damage a common cause? People without the right knowledge on a subject should refrain from committing public utterances. As to the publication of books, whatever he spoke is totally misleading. We again repeat that [the] Government behaved discriminatingly with Orissa and neglected its cause, thus pushed Orissa into backwardness ... Hence, we are pained to say that views of Rajendra Baboo are totally unfounded and misleading and all others who support them are simply trying to swim in the fog.[5]

Similarly, Gourishankar firmly opposed the use of the Bengali script for writing Odia and correctly argued that eastern languages like Bengali, Odia, and Assamese were not derivative or dialects of each

other, but were independent languages that had evolved in due course and had a common origin in Sanskrit. Taking issue with an unwarranted praise of a Bengali text *Bidya Sundar*, he sought to prove that *Rasa Kallol*, authored by Dinakrushna Das long before *Bidya Sundar* was written, was much superior in style and manifestly excellent in comparison (Das 1989: 23).

It is important to frame the language conflict in the political context of the region. By supporting Odia, Gourishankar was not being antagonistic to the interest of Bengali; he was merely reiterating the right of a given people for linguistic self-determination. In fact, it must be admitted that despite partisan politics, the thinkers on both sides of the linguistic divide enjoyed a shared cultural space. Bhudev Mukhopadhyay, Madhusudan Rao, Radhanath Ray, and others closely interacted with each other for common cause. As we shall see in the next chapter, *Utkal Dipika* regularly brought exciting news from Calcutta in the realm of science, medicine, and education for the benefit of Odia readers.

Gourishankar was a fervent supporter of the classical literature of Upendra Bhanja. He carried out many reforms in the field of education and social living. He fought for widow remarriage and the rehabilitation of sex workers after the great famine of 1866. Noticing widespread corruption and irregularity in the selection of textbooks, he raised his voice in the pages of *Dipika*. He was ably supported in this regard by Pandit Gobind Rath, Jagan Mohan Lala, and Dinanath Bandopadhyaya.

Apart from many such measures, Gourishankar spearheaded a number of civic projects such as the formation of the Cuttack municipality, supply of piped water in the urban areas, preservation of Odia language in the Sambalpur region, official representation of Odisha at the national level, protection of the Puri temple from government interference, popularization of the cooperative society, introduction of a steamer service between Chandbali and Cuttack, formation of the Orissa Society in 1870, spread of the teaching of music, establishment of the Cuttack Town Hall, hostels for deserving students from needy background, as well as the establishment of a girls' school and hospital in his village in Dikhitpada. He carried out many of these activities under the two organizations called Utkal Sabha and Orissa Association (Das 1989: 8).

Spiritual-minded, Gourishankar was a regular worshipper in the Brahmo temple and nurtured this institution with the help of Jagan Mohan Lala. After an active life, he passed away on 7 March 1917 (Rath 1997: 68; Rath 1989: 13). The note he wrote in his diary on the first day of 1893 sums up his approach to life: 'Thank God for the new year which I entered today—for what purpose is known to Him. May He bless me and bring me to a sense of my duties and responsibilities so that I may move forward to Him and love and respect Him…. my humble prayer on this New Year's day' (Rath 1997: 68).

To what extent did Gourishankar's affiliation to the Brahmo Samaj movement shape his ideological thinking? Although difficult to determine, it should be admitted that the rebellious streak in his personality and his dissenting approach to life, his desire to indigenize local faith and traditions, could be traced to the Brahmo faith he strongly believed in.

Gourishankar's contributions to the community were impressive, and so were his modesty and self-effacement. He was against the building of all forms of memorials for departed souls, and declared: 'What is the meaning of a memorial? The deeds that someone leaves behind, are they not fitting memorials? Can the memorials ever surpass the true deeds that one leaves behind?' (Rath 1997: 69)

Srichandan Singh sums up Gourishankar's life:

Gourishankar needs no introduction in Orissa. Of course at the national level he is not that familiar, as he deserves. The reason is not far to seek. The only reason which can be ascribed to it is that he himself was a silent worker and believed in Karmayoga. His whole life was a long epic of dedication and public service. There was not a single day in his life when he did not devote his time to public service. Work and public service were the motto of his life. Dr. Harekrishna Mahtab, the famous statesman, once remarked that Gourishankar was the father of journalism in Orissa. He was the founder editor and publisher of *Utkal Dipika*, and considered all his work a sacred worship of the motherland. It is he who shaped the modern prose writing, introduced common people's language into the arena of literature, offered us a uniform standard Oriya language in prose, introduced punctuation in writing, started book reviews and criticism in literature, and thus was the first in many things in Orissa. (Das et al. 1989: ii)

Biswanath Kar

Like Gourishankar Ray, Biswanath Kar's life too was intimately linked with the fate of his journal. The latter was born to a Brahmin family on 24 December 1864 in the Mulabasanta village of the undivided Cuttack district of Odisha (Kar 1983).[6] His parents were Narayana Chandra and Baidehi. He received his early education from his village teachers, Govinda Abhadhana and Brajabandhu Kar. With a flair for learning Sanskrit, he became a student in the Middle School of Kuanpal situated on the bank of the river Birupa. In 1876, following the contemporary custom, he got married at the age of 11 to Janaki (aged eight) of Kanchia village in 1876. In 1882, at the age of 18, he joined the Pyari Mohan Akademi, but missed the rare privilege of meeting Pyari Mohan who had passed away on 28 December 1881. While a student at the Akademi, he felt dismayed by the behaviour of one of his teachers and decided, much against his will, to change the institution; he joined the Cuttack Mission High School. It is here that he came in contact with reform-minded missionary—educators like Young Sahib and learnt to overcome man-made barriers based on religion, caste, and community. He became interested in the need for religious reforms.

Adolescence and Education

By then, fifteen years had passed since the establishment of the Brahmo Samaj in Bengal. It must be remembered that the year 1774 marked the birth of Ram Mohan Roy. At the age of 16, Roy mastered Bengali, Sanskrit, Arabic, Persian, Urdu, Hindi, French, Greek, and Latin. Set up as Brahmo Sabha in 1827 in Calcutta, the movement became the Brahmo Samaj in 1829. The prominent members of the Brahmo Samaj in Odisha were Gourishankar Ray and Jagan Mohan Lala. The Cuttack Brahmo Samaj was established in 1869 and Madhusudan Rao took up its leadership.

Biswanath attended the regular sermons given by Madhusudan Rao and came in close contact with him. Losing interest in formal education, the young learner left the Mission High School in the first half of 1885. While looking for a suitable opening for a job, he took up the editing of two journals named *Samaja* and *Samskaraka* and soon his association with the Brahmo Samaj brought him to the public domain. In 1886, he received an offer and joined a school in the Birol village of Jagatsinghpur. While he gained a reputation for his reformatory zeal elsewhere, some others derided him as iconoclastic and godless. Along with his two younger brothers, Lokanath and Bholanath, Biswanath soon created a stir in the region.

A son was born in 1887 to Janaki and Biswanath. Contrary to traditional practice, Biswanath refused to perform the Brahminical rituals. Discarding the emblems such as the sacred thread, he got initiated into the Brahmo Dharma. Leaving his teaching job in Birol, he joined the Mission School at Cuttack for a brief while as an assistant teacher. Invited by Bhakta Kabi Madhusudan, Biswanath joined the town school as the headmaster. In due course this school became the historic Town Victoria High School and finally, the celebrated Bhakta Madhu Bidyapitha.

Biswanath suffered a family misfortune when he lost his two brothers, Bholanath and Lokanath. Urged to take an educated Brahmo girl as a second wife, Biswanath turned down the offer, and said that despite being unlettered, his wife remained a perfect companion to him. It was his bounden duty to educate her in the path that he had chosen for himself. Maltreated in his village because of his rejection of orthodoxy, Biswanath managed to bring his wife, Janaki, to Cuttack after much effort. He was invited to travel to Patna in October 1892 for a Brahmo conference. On 12 October 1892, Janaki gave birth to Narmada, who would make a name for herself in her later life as a woman of letters.

Madhusudan Rao was deeply concerned with the need to publish a good literary journal. Indeed several journals like *Pradipa*, *Madhupa*, and *Asha* had become extinct by then. Thanks to a collective effort by Madhusudan Rao, Fakir Mohan Senapati, Sadhu Charan Ray, Chandra Mohan Maharana, and Krishna Prasad Choudhury, a new journal called *Utkal Sahitya* was born. Initially well run, the journal soon encountered obstacles both literary and material.

Utkal Sahitya Press

Biswanath thought that the long-term answer to the financial problem of the journal lay in setting up a printing press which would give the necessary revenue as well as facilitate the printing of the journal. He obtained patronage from kings and zamindars, and put in his own meagre resources into the venture. On 10 January 1900, the Utkal Sahitya Press was established in Balu Bazar, Cuttack.

Now that the press was set up, Biswanath's main goal was to create a band of loyal and dedicated writers for the journal in order to promote quality literature. Thanks to his support and inspiration, an entirely new generation of writers such as Gopal Chandra Praharaj, Nanda Kishore Bal, Fakir Mohan Senapati, Sashi Bhushan Rai, Ramshankar Ray, Bhikari Charan Patnaik, Kuntala Kumari Sabat, and others made a name for themselves by writing in the journal.

After the birth of Narmada, four other children were born to Biswanath: Mahananda (25 August 1893), Puranananda (10 January 1896), Pratibha (17 November 1898), and Suprabha (2 May 1901). For Biswanath, family life and literary activities went hand in hand along with the freedom struggle. A challenge soon came in the form of the Partition of Bengal movement in 1905. As a result of the pro-longed agitation in the region, in 1912, lieutenant governors were appointed in United Bengal, Orissa, and Chhota Nagpur respectively, while a chief commissioner took charge of Assam. Biswanath became a member of the Orissa–Bihar Council. He insisted on speaking in Odia and impressed the whole gathering. His eloquence was not only confined to the assembly, but encompassed institutions in Cuttack and elsewhere. As a result, he was widely referred to as the 'Surendranath of Odisha'.

Biswanath the Nationalist

Biswanath was greatly inspired by the Swadeshi movement. This was reflected in his entire attire and disposition. He dressed simply in handwoven cotton clothes in the native style. Asked as to why he spurned Western clothing, he replied that he considered dress as symbolic of his nationalism. If the Westerner could not give up his own clothing even in a tropical country, why would he, an Indian, give up his own dress and attire?

For Biswanath alongside nationalism, social reform in the countryside was equally important. Education was lacking in many villages and therefore he set up a higher school, first in his own village, Mulabasanta. Realizing that female education was equally important, he established a girls' school as well. In the schools he was associated with, he endeavoured to bring the children of all castes together. He also set up a night school for adult education. Other innovations soon followed: The Kar family set up a library to which some of the most illustrious writers donated books; he popularized handwritten magazines called *Aloka*, *Jyotsna*, and *Kaumudi* among school and college students.

Biswanath believed in establishing family ties across linguistic barriers and, therefore, gave his daughter, Narmada, in marriage on 15 October 1919 to Jitendra Kumar Biswas who was a munsif in Bengal. The younger daughters, Pratibha and Suprabha, after suitable training, joined the Ravenshaw Girls' school as teachers. Both received education in the famous Bethune College of Calcutta and became supporters of female education in Odisha. They chose to remain single and worked diligently till the end. Pratibha, like Narmada, wrote and translated admirably in the field of interfaith dialogue and female empowerment. Suprabha retired as the inspector of schools after successfully teaching at the Ravenshaw Girls' School, the cradle of female education in the state. Narmada's collection of short stories called *Prasad* was adapted from the tales of Leo Tolstoy. Pratibha, on the other hand, excelled as a short-story writer and columnist in *Utkal Sahitya* and other journals. While the girls blossomed, Biswanath was finding it difficult to get a steady stream of quality writers for his journal. A crisis was manifest in the case of *Utkal Sahitya* by 1920. Radhanath Ray, the iconic Odia writer, passed away in 1908. Madhusudan died on 28 December 1912, and Fakir Mohan on 14 June 1918; three of the best-known contributors to the journal were tragically lost within a short span of time. It must be noted that Biswanath was extremely discerning as an editor and made stringent editorial judgment.

He had a financial arrangement with the owner of the Cuttack Trading Company (CTC), according to which the CTC books were to be printed by the Utkal Sahitya Press. A portion of the building upstairs served as the accommodation of the Kars. Both the press and the residence were rented accommodations and the building was owned by Akula Mishra. Given the escalation of costs, Mishra suggested the construction of a two-storeyed building to take care of the financial needs on a long-term basis. Biswanath received a loan from Mishra and constructed the building in a plot he purchased in Kali Gali, Cuttack. While the construction made progress, the family lived in the nearby Appa Lodge. They moved to the newly completed building one year after Biswanath's demise in 1934.

Biswanath took personal care of the printing undertaken by his press. He engaged experienced proofreaders and every proof copy passed through his hands. If, by chance, errors crept in, he preferred to consign everything to flames and prepare fresh machine proofs. Biographer Krushna Chandra Kar claims to have seen this with his own eyes on a Sunday. Biswanath had been to a prayer meeting at the Brahmo Samaj, Cuttack. He returned to the press and picked up a printed page for close scrutiny. Upon discovering two to three errors in a page, he destroyed the three thousand copies and ordered fresh paper from the market for printing. Krushna Chandra Kar narrates:

It was necessary to get the book *Savitri* printed within the press hours. Manager Kulamani Kar himself read the machine proofs with close attention and began printing. Biswanath returned that day relatively late. Upon arrival, he went straight to the printing machine. He picked up a sheet and spotted two mistakes in a single page. Immediately, three reams of paper were procured from the market and after correction, fresh printing was undertaken. The already printed reams were put on a bonfire in the courtyard. Biswanath stood there gazing till the entire lot was reduced to ashes. Unfortunately, not a single press in Cuttack emulated the printing idealism of Biswanath. (Nepal 1984: 91)

Biswanath was independent both in thought and action. He was not convinced about the Civil Disobedience Movement and therefore, opposed it at a great cost to his reputation. At the same time, when the British government honoured him with the title of Rai Bahadur, he turned it down.

Life Values

Speaking about his approach to life, he wrote:

The main thing is that I am always in favor of a balanced approach to life. I cannot accept any excess regarding anything. That is why I have developed differences with many people in life. It is futile to expect that life will ever be empty and the heart seldom empty and the heart rarely bereft of joy. I have faced an empty patch in life, but I have never given up hope. What is the alternative other than prayer? Solitary worship, simple prayer, melodious music, and noble companionship—only these can be a remedy to an empty life. I have believed in this approach and have been greatly benefited by it. (Nepal 1984: 32)

Endowed with a strong moral vision of life, he was against superstition and blind beliefs and used *Utkal Sahitya* as an instrument for carrying out the necessary reforms in society. The satirical writings of Nanda Kishore Bal and Gopal Chandra Praharaj that he published in *Utkal Sahitya* came handy for this purpose.

What were the defining features of *Utkal Sahitya* that Biswanth Kar founded and nurtured for long? The journal brought in a variety of genres: essays, criticism, stories, novels, travelogues, life stories, biographies, and autobiographies in an extraordinary manner. Two columns were extensively used: 'Bibidha Prasanga', (Miscellaneous Topics) and 'Sankhipta Samalochana' (Brief Criticism). The journal witnessed the evolution of the Odia prose.

Many notable essays appeared in the Utkal Sahitya: 'The Place of Literature in National Life' appeared on 27 September 1934, 'Palli Sahitya' (Folk Literature) by Nanda Kishore Bal on 20 May 1936, 'Bibahara Itihasa' (The History of Marriage) by Mohini Mohan Senapati on 16 July 1913 and 16 November 1913, 'Krushaki Jiban' (The Life of a Peasant) by Mrutyunjay Rath on 20 March 1911, 'The Value of Education' by Godabarisha Mishra in 1911, 'Adarsha O Unnati' (Ideals and Development) by Ratnakar Pati on 22 November 1919, and 'Education of the Masses During Ancient and Medieval Times' on 23 February 1919. Biswanath had a fruitful literary correspondence with Gangadhar Meher as evidenced in his letters dated 8 March 1896, 15 May 1897, 25 September 1897, 18 August 1899, 25 January 1900, 22 March 1911, 28 March 1911, and 20 November 1914 (Nepal 1984: 38–46).

Utkal Sahitya contained essays of different kinds such as the descriptive, narrative, and reflective ones, as well as essays that were critical and informative. The prominent writers were the following: Fakir Mohan, Radhanath, Madhusudan, Ramshankar, Gangadhar, Krishnaprasad, Chandramohan, Nandakishore, Gopal Chandra, Jagabandhu Singh, Sashi Bhushan, Mohini Mohan, and Jalandhar Dev.

Biswanath followed a spiritual life in a steadfast manner. He offered worship and prayer five times a day. Despite a healthy life, he experienced for the first time an acute pain in the stomach in August 1934 and was confined to bed. On 19 October 1934, he passed away after an eventful life in the service of the Odia language and literature. By the time he died, there was a decline in the circulation of the journal. According to Bhagirathi Nepal, Utkal Sahitya got delinked from the nationalistic forum, and therefore lost readership. But it had already made its mark and served a historical purpose.

After the passing away of Biswanath, his son Mahananda managed the journal for a few years until his untimely death. His son Sunanda revived the journal for a while in the seventies. With his death, the curtain came down on one of the most illustrious chapters in the history of the Odia periodical press, but the journal left a lasting legacy.

We have in Gourishankar and Biswanath two outstanding editors whose mission and goals were different, and yet, both believed in a common cause. Both were the champions of the Odia language and literature, and both shared close family and literary–cultural ties with Bengal. Both belonged to the Brahmo Samaj, and both rejected a narrow sectarian approach to faith and religion. Both were staunch believers in local and indigenous traditions. The deeply syncretic approach to human life they cherished shaped their thinking as editors. Politically, both were moderates, and yet when circumstances demanded, they did not hesitate to take on the state machinery in order to defend the cause of a free press. Their lives inevitably shaped the ideology of the journals they ran.

Gourishankar knew that the best way of preserving press freedom was to have independent finances and therefore, he established the Cuttack Printing Company which supported substantially the running of *Utkal Dipika*. It was set up in the drawing room of Jagmohan Ray. Given the circumstances of the times, and the lack of awareness of such ventures, it was an extraordinary move; farsighted, which revealed that sound finances were responsible for the running of a good periodical press. Subscriptions and advertisements also added to the revenues. By all accounts, the journal was commercially successful.

The two journals zealously guarded their press freedom, and did not compromise with the forces that attempted to subjugate them. They fought a number of court cases and came out of them successful. Gourishankar faced greater challenges since his was a news magazine that took up pressing issues that were administrative and political in nature. Besides, he also championed literary issues that brought his journal in close conflicts with some of the influential Bengali administrators. His best ally, in this regard, was a fair judiciary. Similarly, Biswanath was staunch in his opinion and steadfastly defended his contributors to *Utkal Sahitya*. It must be said that both the editors were balanced in their judgment, and never allowed the pages of their journals to be used for malicious or scurrilous purposes. Ultimately, the credibility of the journals also came to their rescue from being proscribed by authorities.

In large measure, the success of the efforts of Gourishankar and Biswanath lay in the manner in which they were able to persuade the British administrators and the native royalty to be part of their mission. This required tact, intelligence, goodwill, and sincerity of purpose. Alongside, they were able to appeal to the larger society because the community felt that the journals were fearlessly championing the educational, literary, and political interests of the common man.

In the next chapters, we shall examine the content and ideology of the two journals.

Notes

1. I am indebted to Pandit Mrutyunjay Rath for much of the biographical information used in this chapter. See also Das et al. (1989). For a contemporary reception to the memory of Gourishankar, see Singh et al. (1999). All translations from Odia used in the text, unless otherwise indicated, are by me.

2. *Utkal Dipika*, 13 March 1869.

3. *Utkal Dipika*, 13 March 1869, pp. 35–6.

4. *Utkal Dipika*, 13 March 1869, p. 6.

5. *Utkal Dipika*, 13 March 1869.

6. For much of the information regarding the life of Biswanath Kar, I am indebted to *Bagmi Biswanath* by Krushna Chandra Kar. See also Nepal (1984).

3

Print Journalism and Odia
Modernity: *Utkal Dipika*

During the famine, a correspondent had said that henceforth there
would be no problem to fill in the pages of the newspapers. For,
there would be a surfeit of news regarding flood and famine.
—*Utkal Dipika*, 4 September 1869

The epigraph to this chapter sums up justly the nightmare of all editors: how to fill up the pages of a periodical, week after week? Such anxieties, hitherto unknown to a primarily agrarian social order, would become increasingly current in a knowledge society, governed by the desire for information literacy. The assurance by the anonymous correspondent of *Utkal Dipika* was timely. For, by the middle of the nineteenth century, the neighbouring city of Calcutta had begun to experience a vibrant print culture whose effects were being felt in the regions.

Basing on some of the insights offered earlier in the Introduction, I shall look closely in this chapter at the contents of *Utkal Dipika* and critically examine them in the light of the ideology of the colonial/ alternative modernity. It may be useful, in the first instance, to offer a brief outline of the history of this journal.

A Chequered History

Utkal Dipika ran from 1866 to 1937. It continued to be published many years after the founder–editor passed away on 7 March 1917. Begun primarily as a popular medium for the discussion and dissemination of news related to the devastating Odisha Famine of 1866 (Mohanty 1982; Patra 1971), it soon outgrew its primary objective and became a carrier and compendium of news and views from far and near that few newspaper–periodicals of the region could surpass then and now. From the beginning till the death of its founder, *Utkal Dipika* championed the linguistic, cultural, and economic interests of the Odias. It spearheaded a powerful regional–cultural movement. For strategic reasons, it carefully eschewed the politics of the national freedom struggle that had taken roots in different parts of the country after the formation of the Indian National Congress, and lent its faith to the reformist and socially emancipatory agenda. While it regularly carried a column called 'Calcutta Gazette', it avoided all mention of the Bengali militant nationalism that was born in the first decade of the twentieth century. Neither the Alipore Bomb Case (1906–1909) nor the Indo-German Conspiracy case linked to the legendary Jatindranath Mukherjee, also known as Bagha Jatin, who became a martyr in Chashakhand, Balasore, while carrying out military action against the British, were prominently covered in its pages. In this sense, not only Gourishankar and *Utkal Dipika*, but the dominant political narrative of Odisha from 1866 to 1920 seems to run parallel to the one that upheld the anti-British freedom struggle in other parts of the country (Acharya 1989; Das 1998; Dash 2005; Dash 1971; Mallick 2004). It is only after 1920 that the two streams, namely the aspiration for Odia linguistic–cultural unity and the movement for national independence would intersect. The direction that *Utkal Dipika* and Gourishankar gave resulted in the Utkal Union Conference (Utkal

Sammilani) of 1905 and eventually led to the formation of the Odia-speaking political formation called Odisha on 1 April 1936 (Chandra 1982: 1278–85).

How did colonial modernity find a foothold in Odisha? How was it influenced by its Bengali counterpart? What role did the newly emerging bourgeoisie and literati play in generating and disseminating this modernity? How did it impact the life of the ordinary people, the various skilled and unskilled sections of a primarily agrarian social order? Some of these issues will engage our attention in this chapter.

The Genesis

To begin with, we must consider the immediate socio-economic circumstances that led to the founding of the journal. Although Odisha was affected by a series of famines right up to the end of the nineteenth century, the infamous famine of 1866 popularly known as Na-anka Durbhikha, in the ninth regional year of King Divya Singha Deva of Puri, remains a watershed event that left a permanent scar on the Odia psyche. Roughly one-fourth of its population is reported to have perished in the famine. The failure of the monsoon in 1865, unwise export of grain, insufficient awareness of the food grain needs of the populace, inability to import grain in time, unavailability of roadways and waterways, and the hoarding of stock—all of them contributed to the crisis. When help came, shipments could not be brought into the interior. By the end of May 1866, monsoon had set in and by September, large sections were badly affected by cholera and malaria. In the following year, excessive rain caused floods[1] which caused the ruination of rice crops. Approximately, 40,000 tons of rice was imported at an excessive price.

The Odisha famine of 1866 has been well studied by W.W. Hunter and C.E. Buckland. Following the decision of the secretary of state, a famine commission was appointed under the chairmanship of George Campbell who submitted a report on 6 April 1867. The Campbell Commission made a thorough study of the factors that led to the tragedy. It recommended the immediate movement of transport and communication, the building of roads and waterways primarily through the coastal canal system, and the security of tenure for cultivators, and irrigation. An early completion of a trunk road from Calcutta to Cuttack was suggested. As historian Ganeswar Nayak (2009: 1) writes:

Before 1866, in Cuttack district, there were 80 miles of district roads and in Puri district 74 miles. The Commission gave the utmost priority to the development of roads in Orissa, recommending that imperial and local needs to be surveyed as early as possible and funds be assigned for their maintenance and repair. In the post-famine period, some important provincial roads (connecting one province to another) were developed, the most important of which—from a commercial and administrative perspective—was the Cuttack Trunk Road which lies partly in Balasore and partly in Cuttack and runs across eight major rivers.[2]

As a result of these measures post 1866, the communication system greatly improved. After 1887, adds Nayak (2009: 1):

The District Boards of Cuttack, Balasore, Puri were constituted and assumed responsibility for the construction, repair, and maintenance of all classified roads. In 1912 Orissa had 80 miles of metal roads, 850 miles of unmetalled roads, and 698 village roads. By 1933, just prior to becoming a separate province, Orissa had 664 miles of metal roads and 1652 miles of unmetalled roads.

Demographic and Economic Consequences of the Famine

The demographic and economic consequences of the Orissa famine have been well analysed by scholars like Bidyut Mohanty (1993).[3] She discusses scientifically various factors such as the immediate causes of the famine, role of expectation, role of the government, relief policy, different estimates of mortality, famine, sex differences in mortality and outmigration, occupational structures of famine victims, reasons for such suffering, long-term consequences, changes in production relations, organization of agriculture, and post-famine wages and prices, and concludes:

The Orissa famine of 1866 was due to both decline in agricultural output and decline in the income of many classes of people. The prices rose by four to five times compared to the pre-famine years, but were not very much higher than the neighboring famine affected districts like Midnapur and Ganjam ...

The intense suffering in the famine of 1866 had shaken the revenue officials and the relief policy adopted in the famine of 1866 formed the cornerstone of the later famines. So when the Bengal–Bihar famine of 1873–74 was apprehended the revenue department officials tried to save as many people as possible ... As a result there was not much loss of life during the famine of 1873–74.[4] (p. 63)

The main aim of giving this socio-economic background is to underline the circumstances that marked the launching of the journal. For a fairly long time, the pages of the journal acted as valuable and some of the most reliable sources for the history of the Odisha famine of 1866. The immediate reason for starting the journal was to disseminate news regarding the famine among the concerned citizenry and the ruling class.

Opening Issue of the Journal

The printed copies and issues of *Utkal Dipika* lie scattered in the archives and libraries of Odisha, and outside the state. Bansidhar Mohanty's compilation called *Eighteen Sixty Six* (1978) gives us a useful background to the journal and its making while highlighting its cultural significance. Much of the history of the printing press in Odisha and the individuals associated with the founding of *Utkal Dipika* has been provided in Chapter 2 of this volume.

The opening issue of the journal does bring in, from time to time, other events of socio-cultural and educational significance. But on the whole, the issues of 1866 are devoted primarily to the coverage of the famine. For instance, *Utkal Dipika*'s issue dated 11 August 1866 speaks of the 'Famine and the Attitude of People of Calcutta' (p. 27). It brings a graphic account from 'ground zero', as it were, and reports the tragedy as it engulfs the victims:

People are so badly disoriented that, none shares happiness or enthusiasm regarding anything else. The rich or the poor—all have one constant refrain, namely rice. Because of the acute shortage of rice, entire families are facing the threat of extinction. Although many face the crisis, they will be helpless unless they find a way out of this terrible impasse. (p. 21)

The reporter/editor gives details about the community kitchen opened for the destitute and discusses the widespread nature of the famine that spread from Hooghly, Bankura, and Medinipur. He commends the generosity of philanthropic-minded Bengalis who took care of the needy Odias who had travelled to faraway Bengal for help. The references constantly made to Bengal, alongside Odisha, makes it amply clear that regardless of nativistic compulsions, the editor takes into account the interest of the entire Odia- and Bengali-speaking people. In fact, as we shall see, news from Calcutta was a sine qua non in each issue of *Dipika*.

New Editorial Ethics

The credit given to 'philanthropic-minded Bengalis' in *Dipika* makes it amply clear that the editor did not suffer from parochial considerations; he gave credit wherever due purely on objective grounds. The attempt to be 'balanced' and 'even-handed' by the editor is carefully designed to counteract the partisan politics of the colonial state that believed in the 'divide-and-rule' policy. Consciously assuming a moral and ethical tone while discharging one's responsibilities as an editor and activist, may be contrasted with the duplicity and fraudulence of the colonial administration. In the eyes of their readers and the ruled, Gourishankar and Biswanath positioned themselves as honourable men of letters who built an alternative ethics and professionalism; one might say, an alternative modernity. If the ruling class choose to be venal and perfidious, let them be so, we will not stoop down to their level; instead, we will set up better and superior standards in matters of personal and professional conduct—this seems to be the spirit of the refrain, which apparently ensured considerable success for the two editors.

Most of the details of the famine given in *Dipika* are harrowing. Facts seem to be stranger than fiction. The issue number 2, dated 11 August 1866, offers an account that shows human depravity. *Dipika* narrates:

We have recently come to know that one starving woman has entered the village of Mahanga. She seems to be abnormally fond of human flesh. She avoids food readily available and goes to the village cremation ground to dig out corpses from the ground for eating. Once, a beautiful girl was wandering in the village courtyard. Finding her alone, the monster dug her teeth into the flesh. Hearing her cry, people rushed to save her. The woman was given a hot iron treatment for her crime.

For the first time in the history of the medium in Odisha, the journal brings an eyewitness account on the subject with all its vivid and dramatic details such as the above. The purpose was largely to sensitize the administration as well so that immediate corrective steps could be taken.

Other topics find a treatment in the following issues: role of famine committees and their unsatisfactory style of functioning, news of famines in Madras and Bhagalpur, prices and postage details of *Dipika*, list of help received, letters received, the sale of rice by the government, weekly news, theft of documents in the government office, portrait of Sir Harvey Rickett, community kitchen for the destitute, the result of exports abroad, appeal for being excused from revenue payment, issues regarding income tax, system of help, famine in the countryside and the East India Irrigation and Canal Company. Other matters also find place in the subsequent issues. They comprise the question of future land settlements, who gains in the absence of the payment of revenue tax, the attitude of native clerks, future of the beggars, school education, the travel of Bengali youth to England, the setting up of the famine commission, and Agra Durbar. The inventory of the items covered is truly amazing.

Response to the Famine

The additional issue of *Dipika*, dated 8 December 1866, takes up a number of topics such as the question of permanent settlement, the enquiry commission for the famine appointed by the secretary of state, the market for rice, the plan for the next year, the misuse of position and welfare of the nation. It raises twenty-three pertinent questions that clearly reveal the nature and causes of the crisis.

After listing the twenty-three questions, *Utkal Dipika* asks as to how many have read the play *Durbhika* by Babu Gopal Chandra Haldar, a book which is in short supply. Notably, the book does not cover adequately the extent of the famine in the rural areas, nor is the fact widely known that the terrible calamity emptied entire villages of men and women.

The editor of *Dipika* exposes the anti-Odia attitude of Babu Haldar who maintains that the Odias, by definition, are basically an indolent and a complacent lot. Once their needs are satisfied, they hardly bother about their future. Such generalizations, Gourishankar observes, are clearly without any basis. Haldar levels similar charges against the natives that they do not complain to the government well in time. 'Isn't it the government itself and those working under it that are expected to find out about the condition of the people?' asks the editor of *Dipika*. As to the declaration that the Bengali zamindars had assisted adequately, *Dipika* rejects the claim outright, and states that the rich Bengali zamindars like Ramnath Ray Choudhury and Babu Debendranath Thakur had not helped in proportion to their means. On the other hand, some Odia zamindars were unnecessarily held up for blame. In addition, *Dipika* points out a number of factual errors in Haldar's book.

The discussion over the book by Haldar touched a raw nerve among the natives, and Gourishankar was perfectly aware of this angle. The internal colonization of the Odias by the Bengali-dominated administration was likely to thwart much of the efforts made by the British rulers based in Calcutta and Cuttack. However, the British rule itself was enmeshed in a set of contradictions and could not respond expeditiously to the crisis at hand. Colonial modernity was benevolent only in theory.

Running the Journal: the Challenges

As a periodical appearing every week in the printed form and carrying news items of interest to a wide cross section of readers in the region, *Utkal Dipika* must have posed a formidable challenge to its editor and managers. The problem of acquiring the right kind of paper, designing, typesetting, and producing the print run was one part of the challenge; the other must have been the collection of news and advertisements for revenue; the third related to the question of the writing of editorials and columns.

We have insufficient information regarding all the three aspects. It must be noted that the newspaper industry was still in its infancy, and in Odisha, the necessary manpower and infrastructure hardly existed. Most of the advertisements for a long time came from small-time business houses and pharmaceutical companies from Bengal that were into the sale of hair oil, cosmetics, watches, and clocks. They had their head offices in Calcutta. Much later after 1900, we begin to see advertisements for products and services that originated in Odisha. Again, what about the correspondents and journalists? Who were they and what was their background? What remuneration was paid to them? We have no information regarding such aspects, just as we have no concrete idea about the identity of those who wrote columns such as 'Calcutta Gazettes' or 'Saptahik Samachar' (Weekly News Roundup). Unlike a literary journal like *Utkal Sahitya* where the editor could hope to find and publish a collection of literary pieces on a regular basis, the challenge of a news magazine was clearly far greater. Were the editorials written mostly by the editor Gourishankar as they were believed to be so? In that case, it must have been a herculean task, given the fact that the editor himself was a man of town who also doubled up as a social reformer and activist. Besides, a number of verbal and administrative skirmishes were noticed in the pages of *Dipika* regarding the use of the Bengali language. Many of the contestants were well-to-do Bengali administrators with ready access to funds as well as administrative and political power. In a number of instances, *Dipika* was also dragged to court in the alleged defamation cases regarding the 'objectionable' use of language. That *Dipika* came out from such controversies with flying colours is beside the point. What must be noted is the enormous amount of time and resources devoted to fighting such cases; consequently much less time would be left for the editor to run the weekly. Given such constraints, it is nothing less than a miracle that a journal of this kind ran from 1866 to 1937 whereas many periodicals with impressive pedigree perished on the way. The dedication, idealism, and ability of the editor must be the major reason for the success of such a venture. Added to that, was the clear case of patronage of a wider readership that regularly lent its ears in a sustained manner week after week. The credibility of the periodical and the sincerity with which the editorial responsibilities were discharged for a worthy cause were never in doubt. The cause was eminently cultural. It would be a matter of debate whether the British administrators in Odisha and Calcutta were taken in by the profession of loyalty and supplication; that is beside the point. What was important is that both sides gained from this arrangement.

Content, Form, and Ideology

The mast of *Utkal Dipika* in Odia said that it was a 'Saptahik Sambad Patrika'. True to its name, it remained a faithful carrier of news and views. Poems and small skits appeared now and then, but primarily as supplements to the news items. The weekly chronicled news of a variety of activities and reported news of a cross section of society of the coastal districts as well as the Gadjat kingdoms. Announcements and advertisements regarding jobs—both police and civilian—were plentiful and so also for tutors to teach young princes.

In the immediate aftermath of the famine, on 2 January 1969 *Dipika* reported under the heading 'Export of Rice Abroad' and said that 'according to the famine commissioner, as long as trade communication with Odisha had not improved, the export of rice was not to be undertaken'. Similarly, *Dipika*, dated 6 February 1869, reported about the 'help rendered to famine affected people in Ajmer'. News items and columns of *Dipika* could be divided into a few broad categories. Some dealt with controversies like the language debates (Bengali versus Odia) that were continued for many issues. The matter was clearly emotive and touched a raw nerve among the native Odias. The question of the use of the Bengali *lipi* (script) for Odia was a perpetual controversy in the journal.

Janus-faced

The news of travelling circuses, wrestlers, magicians, and photographers were a regular feature as well as announcements regarding debating societies and town-hall lectures. The weekly ran a regular engagement column regarding public events like exhibition of merchandise and assortment of fruits and vegetables from far and near.

By bringing in news regarding the goods and services connected with 'civilized living' such as cosmetics and hair oil, and espousing leisure activities like travelling circuses, still photography, and debating clubs, *Dipika* simultaneously upheld colonial modernity and offered resistance to it, the latter often through acerbic comments about the modern lifestyle of the rich and the profligate. Drinking, in particular, was derided and castigated as an unmitigated curse, an inalienable part of 'Western' education and modernity. Not entirely mistaken if one were to think of Derozio's Young Bengal Movement. Fakir Mohan's iconic story 'Patent Medicine', referred to earlier in the book, is a classic example of this trend. That the author himself was an avid exponent of alternative/vernacular modernity, rooted to sound ethical values, while being a party to habitual drinking, alone and in the company of comrades, as recorded in his memoir, is beside the point. In fact, he served several 'masters' at the same time—championing the downtrodden and the dispossessed on the one hand, and serving the feudal lords and the royalty of Keonjhar and other princely states on the other. If the personal is political, then Fakir Mohan's personal life and politics must be seen in the larger context of the colonial modernity project. The espousal of a set of contradictory values at the same time could only be the result of a complex ideology of which he and others were products. Those who idealize Fakir Mohan and gloss over his moral 'flaws', or see them as incompatible with the 'progressive' nature of his writings must see the answer in the colonial situation.

News roundup covered interesting tidbits from far and near. International news brought tidings of war from Europe and South Africa just as 'Calcutta Gazettes' disseminated interesting cultural items from Calcutta.[5] A typical issue of the journal on 6 February 1869 carried the following features:

(a) Weekly news
(b) Letters received
(c) Population of Bengal
(d) Laws regarding legal separation
(e) Income tax
(f) Character of policemen
(g) Rates of rice at Balasore, Jaleswar, Jagatsinghpur, Puri, and Cuttack

Similarly, *Dipika*, dated 10 July 1869, spoke on '*Bidhaba Bibaha*' (Widow Remarriage) and wrote: 'We had earlier published news about widow remarriage in Bombay. We would now like to inform our readers that such a marriage is quite new in Bombay. For the first time ever, Vidyasagar's message has found its target. One can imagine the reaction of conservatively inclined aged Hindus to such developments.'

Dipika and Affairs of the Colonial State

It should be noticed that in choosing to cover much of the above items and features, *Dipika* sought to align itself with the format of a model English journal/periodical brought to India by the English and Irishmen as we have seen in Chapter 1. After all, items such as weekly news, the letters received, the population of regions, the laws regarding legal separation, income tax, the character of policemen, and the rates of rice in different towns and cities—these must be an inventory fairly new to a traditional society. Modern newspapers and periodicals depend on the revenue administration in the form of advertisements. Consequently, much of the space in the journals and weeklies must be taken by news related to the affairs of the colonial state.

The colonial administrative system in India generated a bureaucracy to handle the taxation system. Communicating with the clients regarding the tax policies became an important aspect of the Raj. We see a considerable coverage of these aspects in *Dipika*. For instance, we find that the manual about the water tax finds a place in *Dipika*, dated 10 July 1869. The notice of the High Level Canal of Odisha stating the rates for the agriculturalists of Cuttack, Tangi, Bairi, and Nailupur, appears in the issue dated 28 May 1870. Public debates about the merits of vaccination against small pox appeared in the weekly dated 19 February 1870. It is worth noting that the Western (allopathic) system of medicine and treatment was increasingly gaining ground. Lessons in hygiene were imparted by missionaries in the educational institutions run by them. There was predictably a resistance to such remedies in interested circles and vested interests. Quacks of various kinds and obscurantist elements in all communities that thrived in sorcery and witchcraft were against the introduction of the scientific system of medicine. It must be admitted in the context that the state appears to have played little or no supportive role for the indigenous system like the Ayurveda. No such evidence, at any rate, is found in the pages of *Dipika*. The colonial state clearly did not play an aggressive role in matters of personal hygiene and medical ethics.

It is primarily through its many reports and dispatches that *Utkal Dipika* brought to the attention of its readers important developments taking place in the region and elsewhere. For instance, the spread of education in Deogarh finds mention in *Dipika* dated 24 October 1908. The functioning of the Ravenshaw Girls' School is commended in its issue of 18 January 1908, just as the establishment of the Cuttack Engineering School is hailed in the issue dated 26 January 1908. The meeting of the Muslim Educational Society at Dhamnagar, in Bhadrak, is held up for special praise in the issue dated 25 January 1908. Likewise, concern is expressed for the ending of law education in Odisha in *Dipika* dated 18 January 1908.

There are differences to this rule as well. In the issue of 10 July 1869, *Dipika* focused attention on the contentious issue of 'Writing Odia Script in Bengali' and wrote:

Last week Babu Umacharan Haldar published a long journal whose aim is to produce Odia books and journals through the Bengali scripts. The argument is frankly staggering and beyond us. The idea was that since the Odia script was written with the help of Bengali pen and ink, is it not logical to infer that it should be written through the Bengali script?

It added tongue in cheek: 'If our readers are not aware of [the]origin of paper, pen and ink, then they must remember that these were created in Bengal.' Language politics at one level seems to be the result of ethnic prejudice and rivalry. However, on closer look, it would be clear that this was largely a product of the colonial administration. The preference given to the Bengali gentry and babus owing to their education in the Hindu and other colleges and Calcutta University, for employment in the outlying provinces like Odisha, Assam, and Bihar must be seen as part of the colonial modernity project. Gourishankar's journal is seen to uphold this modernity while attempting to critique it with the help of an alternative. This contradiction or rather the simultaneity of the colonial and the anti-colonial was ingrained in the situation; the journal merely reflected and refracted this reality.

Ill-treatment of the natives and atrocities of the British officials are reported from time to time. These include instances of misdemeanour, both bureaucratic and sexual. *Dipika's* issues of 15 September 1866 and 29 December 1866 outline examples of such evils, and seek corrective action from the higher authorities. The issue dated 22 September 1866, on the other hand, draws attention to the generosity of Queen Victoria in helping an old man in England, as reported in the *Hindu Patriot*. At the same time, while thanking the missionaries for arranging a community kitchen for the hungry and the homeless, *Dipika* is firm that the able-bodied should desist from free food. It advises the authorities accordingly in its issue dated 17 November 1866. In the issue dated 1 December 1866, it commends the Bengali youth for seeking higher education in England, and castigates the Odia counterparts for their laziness and indolence. 'Why do the Odias give up all desire for learning the moment they leave school?' it asks pointedly.

Colonial Modernity and Discursive Public Space

A major activity in which the colonial gentry in Odisha participated was the making of an intellectual and discursive public space.

Forums such as the Brahmo Mandir, school premises and town halls, etc., became the favoured venue for public lectures, discussions, and debates. Many of the advocates and practitioners of the town hall lectures/debates were Bengalis domiciled in Odisha; some of them were Bengali officials who were temporarily posted in the region. Yet others were intellectually gifted Odias who considered it important to spearhead such efforts for the benefit of their brethren. By the late nineteenth century, a number of debating clubs had sprung up in Cuttack. The professorate at Ravenshaw College played an active part in the creation of a new generation of intellectual leaders. A number of Ravenshaw dons were educated abroad and brought with them a new culture of learning. The discussion about primers written in English and patterned after the Western models finds frequent mention in the pages of *Dipika*. For instance, while the issue of January 1899 features a full-page advertisement welcoming the arrival of Lord Curzon, it also carries an announcement that 'Oriya Arithmetic by Mrs. J.B. Rae can be had from an application to Miss H.K. Leigh, Cuttack and the Reverend George Hamber B.A. Balasore'. The same issue of the journal announces the results of the middle-school examinations and publishes a list of successful students, a practice that would continue as a regular feature.

Under 'Public Engagements', *Dipika*, dated January 1869, issues the following notice:

The first anniversary meeting of the Cuttack Debating Clubs will be held at the High School Theatre on Friday the 12th instant at 7.00 pm when Baboo Jaggomohun Roy will read a paper on 'The Last Year's Progress of the Club.'

Cuttack, The 5th February 1869
O.C. Chatterjee, Hony. Secretary, C.D. Club

Another notice, dated 5 August 1869, announces the holding of a lecture by Babu Rajkrishna Mukherjee on 'The Life and Doctrine of Buddha' at the High School Theatre on 11 August 1869. The notice appears in *Utkal Dipika* dated 7 August 1869.

Similarly, a notice of the club, date marked 9 February, announced:

Public Engagement

The Cuttack Debating Club Lecture on 'Debating Clubs' by T.M. Kirkwood
Esq. C.S. on Wednesday the 24th instant at 7.00 pm.

Cuttack   Abhinash Chandra Chatterjee
9th February 1869   Hony. Secretary. C.D. Club

While the Indians spoke on different topics in the Cuttack Debating
Club, T.M. Kirkwood Esq. chose to (or was requested to) speak on the
importance of debating clubs. Presumably the idea was to impress the
audience about the fact that as a Western practice, it was part of the
larger intellectual tradition that the West could legitimately be proud
of. No report unfortunately exists about the contents of Kirkwood's
lecture. But it can be safely assumed that he would have begun with
the Greek tradition of dialogues, beginning with *The Republic* of Plato.
    Another notice date marked 20 July 1870, Cuttack, informs the
readers of *Utkal Dipika*:

Baboo Rajkrishno Mookerjee will speak on 'Hindu mythology' at Young
Men's Literary Association to be held at the premises of Baboo Luckhmee
Narayan Roy Choudhury on Sunday 31st at 8.00 pm.

Bhagavati Charan Chatterjee,
Young Men's Literary Association.

Similarly, there is an announcement for a lecture to be delivered on
'The State of Education in Orissa' by Babu Dwarakanath Chukroburty
at the Cuttack Debating Club. Both the Odias and the non-Odias,
including Bengalis, are seen to actively participate in the public forums
such as the town hall meetings and public lectures. However, since
the activity required skill and training, most speakers tended to come
from the higher echelons of education, judiciary, and administration;
the objective in many cases was to promote the virtues of civic life in
the West, that is, to support the colonial modernity project.

Colonial Sports and School Drills

Nor was the concept of physical education of the Western type lacking; while wrestling in the *akhada* (wrestling ground) and native games continued, a new feature introduced in the schools, was the school drill. Several issues of the journal featured through advertisements, the arrival of new books that claimed to teach in an innovative manner, drills to school children. One by Bhagabanchandra Singh that finds mention in the issue dated 17 June 1899 is a good example, but clearly not the only one of its kind. Of similar kind was the Western practice of taking and preserving family or group photographs, a practice that had become current by the middle of the nineteenth century in Bengal. An announcement for family photographs in a studio is seen in *Dipika*'s issue dated 22 July 1899.

Winds of Change: Home and Abroad

The introduction of Western education, medicine, healthcare, agriculture, canal system, engineering, mathematics and science, the reading of English, the classics and the European literature are growingly seen as the gift of the Raj, although *Utkal Dipika* and *Utkal Sahitya* continue to strike a balance with the native tradition.[6] However, royal visits to India are uniformly greeted with joy. For instance, *Dipika* dated 8 January 1870, expresses happiness for the visit of Lord Mayo in 1869 (who was tragically assassinated by a convict in the Andamans later) and welcomes the visit of the Duke of Edinburgh. It adds: 'After the British occupation of India, no one from the royal family had stepped into this land. The visit of the prince, Duke of Edinburgh, is clearly a major event this year, a landmark indeed in the nation's history.'

While the Western modernity project through debating clubs and town hall lectures went hand in hand with the discussion and circulation of the Odia classics (several notices in the journals, for instance, appeared showing concern about the non-availability of the Odia classics in print), it was clearly through the weekly news column and dispatches from elsewhere that the Odia readers of *Dipika* were urged to be part of the Western modernization project. Women's education and protection of women's rights were considered important and were highlighted, paradoxically at times through inter-religious bigotry. For instance, the Weekly News of *Dipika*, 4 September 1869, chronicles the news of an old *Kazi* (Muslim religious preacher) who got married to a young woman of 18 years: 'Suspecting her fidelity and fearing that she "would go astray", the Kazi tried to keep her under closed doors. At her insistence to visit her parents, he physically assaulted her and burnt her in many parts. The Kazi has been punished and has been suitably jailed for seven years.' Clearly, the editor evades the instances of such maltreatment of young spouses by aged Hindu husbands while singling out the case of the Muslim Kazi.

Western examples of positive role models come handy in this aspect. The West remains the trendsetter. After all, comments *Dipika* of 4 June 1870: 'Cultured America has given emancipated women. There is no difference of gender in the southern State of America. Women there have earned the right to be Jury members.'

Reforms clearly dominated the agenda. There is a prolonged discussion about criminal tribes in the issue of 5 November 1870. The columnist commends the efforts of Stephen Sahib who wishes to pass a bill to regulate the criminal tribe: 'After all, Stephen Sahib claims that *there are very few crimes in the rural areas of England*' [emphasis mine].

While Western culture is a valourized entity and travel abroad constitutes prestige, *Dipika* is not convinced that for the study of Indian languages, that too for a classical tongue like Sanskrit, one has to go abroad. *Dipika*, dated 19 February 1870, reports: 'According to *Daily News*, Pandit Harihar Das of Puri Sanskrit School is an expert in Nyaya Shastra, English, Greek and Latin. We had not known that this matter had proceeded so far. We only know that he had a desire to travel. In the event, Das could travel up to Bombay ...'

While Bengalis and Christians are commended for being more advanced culturally, there is a certain degree of ambiguity expressed vis-à-vis the question of being converted to Christianity. Under the heading 'A Native Widow embraces Christianity', it speaks of Ganesh Sundari Das and adds with a tinge of anxiety: 'There has been a stir among the Hindu community that she has been influenced by a Christian priest and claimed that she was a major and embraced the new religion on her own volition.'

Similarly, reforms like widow remarriage taking place in the neighbouring Bengal are applauded. Under the heading 'Novel Marriage', *Dipika*, in its issue dated 7 January 1869, observes with satisfaction: 'Reading *Som Prakash*, we came to know that recently a widow remarriage took place. Babu Upendranath Das, the son of the advocate of the High Court of Calcutta Ganath Das has got married to Nabakrushna Das. There was a good gathering at the marriage.'

Colonial Science and the Modernizing Agenda

The formation of science societies and scientific developments in India as a result of Western modernity are invariably commended. *Dipika*'s issue dated 25 February 1899, for instance, praises the efforts of Bengali scientists and informs the readers about how to preserve lemon juice without mixing it with wine. It congratulates Scientist Priyanath Das for this singular achievement. Several measures introduced in connection with the canal systems find mention in *Dipika*. On the other hand, in its issue dated 11 December 1869, it speaks of the debate over the merits of a long vacation for school children. In the same issue, it underlines the need to have a proper history textbook for Odisha. It highlights the necessity of having an ideal primer for children, free from superstition, in the issue dated 28 August 1869. On the other hand, the issue dated 29 May 1869 defends the cause of English education. The benefits of an insurance policy, a new idea imported from the West, as a bulwark against unforeseen misfortunes, are seen in the advertisements. For instance, *Dipika*, in its issue dated April 1900, carries an advertisement by a New York insurance company. Signed by H.J. Bell, the company's agent in Cuttack, it promises 'a safe and profitable investment' just as *Easy Guides to Translation from Oria to English* by Biswanath Mishra is advertised in the issued dated 16 September 1899.

Tradition and Modernity

Utkal Dipika endeavoured to maintain a balance between tradition and change; it spoke of the benefits of English education and Westernization, and was at the same time conscious of the baneful aspects as well. Well informed about the latter, it pointed these out for the benefit of the natives wherever it could. Never challenging the English administrative structure and the authorities directly, it sought to negotiate with them; it believed firmly in self-respect and never compromised on this score. This may be visible in several of its editorials, columns and letters to the editors. The anonymous letter dated 11 February 1899, written in English and published at the end of the nineteenth century may be indicative of the editorial stand.

To
The Editor, *Utkal Dipika*

Sir,

I shall be highly obliged if you will kindly publish the few following lines in your esteemed paper...

Receiving a card of invitation signed by Mr. ENGLISH, the Secretary of the late Cuttack Exhibition, I went there on the first day of its opening. While I was going around the exhibits, a Constable came to me to say that I was wanted by Babu Gopal Ballabh Das who was then at one of the entrances to the Show. On my seeing him he kindly (?) advised me to the fact that as I was in my native dress I had better leave the place that the ladies may not be shocked at our hideously indecent dress. One or two other gentlemen were similarly advised. I followed his sage advice and expected to see the place almost emptied as excepting the Europeans and a very few of the native gentlemen this whole assembly were on their national dress. But to my great surprise I found he let many gentlemen—professors, pundits, zamindars, relatives of Raj Bahadoors, graduates, Amlas and others go unmolested although they too were dressed in the native fashion. Will Babu G.B. Das, so well known for his profession and national feeling, explain to the public what induced him to insult gentlemen duly invited when no instruction had been given as to the dress they should appear in, and will the managing committee of the exhibition be good enough to enquire into his strange conduct?

Cuttack   Yours
8.2.99   XYZ

Epilogue

Gourishankar passed away on 7 March 1917. How was his passing received by the contemporary readership, his colleagues, the officials, the reformers, fellow followers of the Brahmo Samaj, and ordinary men on the street and the women at home? It would be interesting to find this out from a journalistic point of view. The fact that the journal continued its journey for the next ten years testifies to its strength and resilience, and the manner in which its editor must have prepared a second-rung leadership. *Dipika* published the issue dated 10 March 1917 when the city of Cuttack was steeped in gloom and sorrow. The obituary that appeared in the issue is worth reproducing:

The late Gourishankar

Gourishankar, the eldest, the most accomplished, the most dedicated and the most notable son of modern Odisha, the brightest star in the constellation, has disappeared from the skies of Utkal. It would be a vain dream to think that we can spot such a stellar orbit again. The one, who managed the Cuttack Printing Press for more than a century, left the earth last Wednesday on 7 March 1917 in the evening hours. He was a most deserving son of Odisha. He has displayed one pointed devotion to work throughout his life. We are unable to narrate the life of this saint at present. We earnestly hope that his nephew Babu Ramshankar Ray will come to our rescue…Gourishankar was involved with many worthy endeavors throughout his life—the printing press of *Utkal Dipika*, the girls' school and hospital at Asureshwara, Pyarimohan Akademi at Cuttack, the Town Hall and the Kayastha Boarding are all emblems of his consecrated life. He strove till his last breath, looking after the printing press, *Utkal Dipika* and Odisha. Today, the land has lost her cherished son. Gourishankar symbolized the pride of Odisha. At the cremation ground at Khannagar, his ashes lie scattered. We get lost in his memories and are unable to put them down on paper. He has departed leaving us disconsolate. And yet his genius and achievements will last forever...

The obituary was a moving tribute and captured the deep sense of sorrow the occasion demanded. It is worth noting, however, that among the things the obituary mentions as part of Gourishankar's legacy is his stellar contribution to Odisha's print culture and female education. Indeed, he inherited a great medium from the colonial state, and used it imaginatively for a collective good to fashion out an alternative modernity in Odisha.

Notes

1. In fact famines and floods have been the fate of Odisha. This would continue for the most part of the nineteenth century. See Karuna Sagar Behera and B.B. Bhatt, 'Devastating Cyclone in Balasore District in 1874', *The Orissa Historical Research Journal (OHRJ)*, XXXIV (3 and 4).

2. For a contemporary sympathetic account of the state of the Odia economy from a British official's point of view, see Toynbee (2005). All translations from Odia into English used in the chapter, unless otherwise indicated, are by me.

3. See also Bolton (1985) and Patnaik (1980).

4. See also G. Nayak (2010). For a representative account of the evolution of the city during the colonial rule in Odisha, see Mohanty (2007).

5. Calcutta has had a lasting effect on the Odia imaginary. See, for instance, J. Nayak (2010).

6. For an excellent rendering of facts into semi-fiction based on the narratives of nineteenth-century Odisha, see Das (1992 and 2004).

4

Utkal Sahitya and Colonial/Alternative Modernity

Notice

After sufficient thought and deliberation, we have undertaken the publication of Utkal Sahitya. We have, in this mission, sought grace and blessings from the Almighty and embarked on our task. We feel little need to write a long introduction in order to explain the significance of a monthly. This has been well explained in the accompanying note of one of our close colleagues.[1]

Western education has brought about many changes in all aspects of our life. Similar developments have taken place in the field of literature. Changes are indeed desirable. Mankind cannot stand still in one place for ever. Immobility is anathema to a living and organic order. It is not the sign of wisdom to uphold tradition at the expense of change. Nor can we give up modernity for the sake of tradition. Only the wise know how to maintain a balance between the two. This is a path shown by wise men of all ages and

*times…. As long as we remain alive, we will continue to follow this
path. The treasure house of Odia literature may not be overflowing
with priceless valuables, but it is not empty either. There is a great
need for creating a new literature. Utkal Sahitya seeks to act as a
representative of both tradition and modernity.*[2]

—*Utkal Sahitya*, inaugural issue, 1897

Editor Biswanath Kar's role was clearly marked out at the inaugura-
tion of the new journal he founded towards the end of the nineteenth
century. He knew he had 'to act as a representative of both tradition
and modernity'—as a cultural mediator between Odisha and the West.
In no small measure was this task different from that of his senior,
Gourishankar Ray, who had founded the weekly *Utkal Dipika* during
the turbulent times in 1866. As it happened, both the editors would
steer, in large measure, the cultural destiny of Odisha steadfastly for
half a century. Both left lasting impressions on the mind and life of
their community. Both carried out their editorial task with dedication
and determination and left behind a legacy through their periodicals
that few could match.

Since our task is not primarily to offer a narrative history of the
journal, but to make a critical analysis of its role with respect to the
modernity project in Odisha, we shall closely examine in this chapter
the manner in which *Utkal Sahitya* dealt with colonial/alternative
modernity in Odisha.

It is worth noting, at the outset, that Chandramohan Maharana, a
close colleague and confidante of Biswanath Kar, wrote a note entitled
'The Usefulness of a Literary Journal' in the inaugural issue of *Utkal
Sahitya*, 1897: 'To seek for knowledge is the uniqueness of human
beings. There are two ways of acquiring knowledge: Anubhava and
Adhyana, namely experience and study. Through careful observation
and judgment, one can enhance the existing body of knowledge. Both
the approaches sustain each other.'[3]

What is striking in this prefatory message, which incidentally serves
partly as the manifesto of the journal, is that both Kar and Maharana,
as editorial spokesmen, are not content to be confined to the format of

the journal which is largely inspired by the West. A literary magazine which is modelled after its Victorian (and later Edwardian) counterparts would be expected to fulfil its mission, especially in its implanted and derivative form, in accordance with the generic practice in Britain. In fact, there were a number of such periodicals in India towards the close of the nineteenth century. *Utkal Sahitya*'s managers seem to be keen that the new journal should chart out an independent path for itself even while sharing a basic affinity with its English models. Therefore, perhaps, is the stress on the Sanskrit terms 'anubhava' and 'adhyayana' which carry connotations deeper than their rough equivalents in English. Indeed, as we shall see, constant efforts were made by Biswanath Kar to give an indigenous turn to the contents and form of the journal.

It has to be admitted that *Utkal Sahitya* actively dealt with the colonial modernity project in Odisha. Developments in the print medium, as well as advancements in communication, including the railways and the telegraphic services across the country brought the middle class readers in the cities and large towns in India increasingly closer to the cultural and social developments in Britain. Costume, dress, lifestyle, food habits and culinary practice, travel and pilgrimage—newer means and modes pertaining to these aspects—percolated down from the metropolis to the smaller towns as they did in Victorian England; they were widely discussed and debated in the journals and periodicals in India as sources of desire and curiosity. This was common to many contemporary journals in Odisha.

New Cultural Codes

The issues that colonial modernity brought to the attention of the emerging cultural elites in India were many, as indicated earlier in this volume. For instance, with the improvement in healthcare and medical facilities, the average lifespan of men increased, and so also the attendant issues hitherto absent in the Eastern context. 'The Danger of Middle Age',—the title of an essay in *Utkal Sahitya* may have resonances in the currently valourized notion of 'health care'. Authored by Shashibhushan Ray, the son of Radhanath Ray, the architect of Odia literary modernism, the article in *Utkal Sahitya*[4] is an interesting study of men's changing attitude to middle age.

Shashibhushan opens his article by asking the following question:

> The longer life span of people noticed earlier is surprisingly not seen today. Many seem to pass away after entering the age of fifty. There has been a spread of education and the average men and the government have a greater awareness of health care. And yet we should perhaps enquire as to why the lifespan of people is getting decreased day by day. (p. 158)

The essayist goes on to analyse reasons that may explain this phenomenon. While death during the middle age seems to be common in all sections, it is particularly noticed, he says, among the more educated citizens. Officials, businessmen, lawyers, physicians, and teachers seem to comprise this group; they are city-based and shoulder responsibility. Nor can they have the luxury of rest after work; the competitive life does not permit this. The sense of responsibility increases when working men have to report to their superiors.

We may see, he says, basically two groups in this context: businessmen and service holders. Further, we may notice the difference between a businessman in the village and his counterpart in the city or town. Doctors and lawyers must satisfy their clients for the sake of their livelihood. Consequently, they have to face increased work pressure and suffer from mental strain. Some of the well-established lawyers of today become legal advisers, others become council members and yet others municipality commissioners and chairmen of district boards. They devote themselves to philanthropic work as well. It has been aptly said that such people do not even have time to die!

Ray argues that such men do not have the luxury of slowing down. They have little or no time for leisure. The hectic pace begins from childhood and adolescence and continues thereafter. Rigorous training of the mind and endless rounds of examinations from an early age lead one to a later life full of anxiety and work pressure. Further, we witness an increased migration of people from the village to the urban areas, full of crowded habitation. The anxiety and excitement of the city life can be lessened by the peace and tranquility prevalent in the village.

On the other hand, excessive smoking and drinking must surely lead to early death.

Thus, as the author sums up, there are five principal reasons for the decline and early death among the educated sections: (a) excessive responsibility, (b) working with anxiety, (c) crowded life, (d) sedentary work culture and finally, (e) intemperate lifestyle. Consequently, many people suffer from the diseases of the heart, lung, and liver as well as from diabetes.

Each of the stages in life such as childhood, youth, old age poses dangers to us. One must therefore remain vigilant about the dangers of middle age. The picture of youth, seen at this period, may be misleading. The onset of the problems gives early indication, such as the inability to sleep, insufficient strength, a sense of fatigue, and the inability to concentrate. On the other hand, there are many people who remain healthy despite carrying out an active life full of responsibilities.

Through a well-structured essay that focuses on a widely perceived problem of death during the middle age, Shashibhushan Ray deals with an important aspect of colonial modernity, one involving the rise in education, declining health care, addiction to smoking and drinking, and increased responsibilities and lifestyle diseases. Arguments are developed logically and systematically, and finally, a solution is given in terms of a life of temperance and ethical conduct. In Ray's essay, we see an interesting discourse on work, leisure, and healthcare in the late Victorian and early modern culture in India. While he himself may not have been articulate about the ideological underpinning in the issue, we may see the essay as part of the anxiety of the colonized elite regarding the cost of Western education. Western education is seen to lead to ambition, long hours of work, unhealthy habits and work culture, and evil practices such as drinking and so on; these have been recurrent refrains in much of the narrative of decline symptomatic of the contemporary discourse. Shashibhushan reiterates this anxiety in his essay about the problem of middle age. The answer he provides is the traditional virtues of temperance and the wisdom of the middle path. Needless to say, there is no real questioning of the modernity project; only the need to find a quick palliative.

Shashibhushan's interesting reflections on disease and healthcare in colonial Odisha are to be seen in the light of the study of the subject by Biswamoy Pati and David Arnold. In his seminal work *Health, Medicine and Empire: Perspectives on Colonial India* (2001), Pati and his contributors speak on the social history of health and medicine in colonial India and highlight Europe's relationship with India's indigenous medical systems. Similarly, in *Colonizing the Body: State Medicine and Epidemic Disease in Nineteenth-Century India* (1993), David Arnold underlines the centrality of the body to political authority, and the vital role of the state in colonial India. Given the pivotal role played by the colonial state in determining the health and illness of the subject, as argued by the two scholars, Shashibhushan's advice of discipline and temperance, for a sound bodily life and longevity, has to be taken in a qualified sense. In fact, as Arnold shows, the colonial state apparatus in India did not have a uniform policy regarding medical treatment and administration; often its approach to healthcare and medical treatment varied according to local circumstances. How, then, can sound health be ensured only by an ethical conduct?

Shashibhushan was an acute observer of culture and an acclaimed travel writer of his times. His travelogue *Dakhinatya Bhramana* (1896 [1921])[5] was a significant text of the intercultural encounter. An important subtext in this travel narrative is the construction of a southern imaginary against which the emerging Odia consciousness could be judged. Despite the affinity the Odia language shares with the Dravidian substratum, Odisha's language and culture are generally perceived as part of the Indo-Aryan stream. Shashibhushan, on the other hand, finds the southern land 'beautiful' in all aspects. Its climate is found to be 'superior' to Odisha's. There are many things 'worth seeing' here. People here are 'endowed with wealth, wisdom, and dignity'. The sculpture and the architecture of its cities are 'unrivalled'. Its rivers like Godavari, Krishna, Kaveri, and Tungabhadra are 'full of natural beauty' (Mohanty 2008: 156). Judged against the colonial status of Odisha, the cultural servility of the Odia elites and their desire for worthy role models, Shashibhushan's journey to the South helps shape the Odia identity (Mohanty 2008: 156) as part of a larger imaginary.

Menace of Plagiarism

The same issue of the journal carries an article on plagiarism. In a tongue-in-cheek manner, the author writes a humorous essay under the title 'Sandarva Harana' (Theft of Treatise). It begins by making a self-evident assertion:

Regardless of the fame of any writer, all may be fairly accused of plagiarism. The writers from the East or the West, all may be guilty of this malady. It can never be treated as objectionable or condemnable. After all, hasn't been well said that 'Kavita, Banita or Lata' (a poem, young lass or a creeper) cannot grow by themselves; they all need some support. This is most certainly true, even in the literal sense. (Ray 1896 [1921]: 162)

The essay, centring on the widespread case of adaptation and translation from the British and European literary sources, is a good instance of the contemporary literary–cultural transaction between India and Britain. No easy answers are found, then as well as now, to the manner in which such matters were to be handled, and settled. How does one deal with the question of 'influence' whereas the instance of outright copying is more easily identified and disfavoured? Needless to say, such questions are not raised by the essayist.

It's remarkable that the issue of plagiarism could be the source of such worry to an audience, much of which was slavish in its approach to Western modernity. The reference to 'Kavita, Banita and Lata' is brought metaphorically from the native sources, perhaps to prove the point, and make literary 'theft' a lesser crime for a colonized people.

Imperialism and War

Several essays in *Utkal Sahitya* deal with political topics that review the international situation; they establish linkages, such as between imperialism and war, integral to understanding Western modernity. Under the same title, Chandrasekhar Mishra, B.L. (Bachelor of Law), unveils the reasons for conflicts among the European nations. Quoting Jackson, he says: 'War is common to imperialism, which is the political expression of monopoly capitalism.' Displaying an in-depth knowledge of developments on the political and military fronts and exploration of issues such as diplomacy, balance of power, and annexation of land by colonial powers, Mishra tells the reader of the imperial designs of nations like England, France, Germany, Russia, Japan, China, Indo-China, Africa, and West Asia. He concludes that it is basically the greed for empire that has prompted the various powers and their conglomerates to embark on war (p. 307).

The essay by Mishra in *Utkal Sahitya* deserves attention for the manner in which it makes a critique of the modernist project: Janus-faced European modernism necessarily leads to violence and war, even as it extols the virtue of progress and civilization. Admittedly, the essayist does not provide an alternative system of politics that could avoid the outbreak of war, but the questioning of the modernity project is a good beginning by itself.

Modernity and New Historiography

If the flip side of the modernity project has been shown by Chandrasekhar Mishra, then the idea of modern historiography gains ground in many essays in *Utkal Sahitya*. It must be noted here that although Odisha had a rich tradition of voyages abroad to far-away lands like Lanka, Java, and Bali, there are very few accounts available, based on historical documentation. Most narratives have been in the realm of legends, folklore, and the oral tradition. This has been largely true of the other regions in India as well. In fact, Western historiography based on a set of empirically verifiable facts, has not been as pervasive in India as in Europe. An astute editor, Biswanath Kar, conscious of his role as a 'modernizer' spearheaded efforts to fill this gap. Consequently, we find in the pages of *Utkal Sahitya*, a number of essays that deal with Odisha's historical past. The article *'Prachina Utkalare Jalajatra'* (Sea Voyages in Ancient Utkal) combines history, myths, legends, and folklores (Mohapatra 1996: 203–21) in order to trace the traditions of seafaring activities in Odisha, but there is little here that can bear scrutiny in empirical terms.

Birupakhya Kar begins the essay by alluding to the rich seafaring tradition of Athens, England and America. There is glory in association, but can such association take us far? He asks a pointed question rhetorically: 'Three parts of India are surrounded by water. Consequently, Indians must be adept in sea voyages. Was India ever a maritime nation? That is not the main objective of this essay. A small part of India, namely Odisha or ancient Kalinga's maritime tradition is the subject of this essay' (p. 265).[6]

Kar outlines the history of Odisha from the earlier period when it stretched from Ganga to Godavari. The objective that he sets before himself is to prove 'the excellence' of Odias in seafaring activities (p. 266).

He alludes to the Buddhist period and the annals of the Buddhist pilgrim Bigyandujtta. Referring to Chanakya's *Arthashastra* in the fourth century AD, he speculates that the voyages mentioned in the book *must surely* refer to Kalinga [emphasis mine]. The shift from Chanakya to Kalinga occurs through qualifiers such as 'perhaps' and 'maybe'. Assertions are made with the help of speculations and surmises. He links the verses from Chanakya to the practices in the Odia villages during the month of Kartika, when women paint their houses and draw the picture of the native ships and worship them.

He then refers to the history of colonization by the Odias during the first century AD. According to him, in 75 AD, the Odias established a colony in Java. Known as Klings, these tribes continue to live in Malaysia and Singapore as well. In his support, he alludes to the accounts of Ptolemy and suggests that the ports mentioned by the Roman historian such as Pakoura, Nanigaina, Katidarmana, Kosamba, Tyndis, Dosaram, and Adamas refer actually to places and rivers like Pakura (near Ganjam), Puri, Cuttack, Kosamba (Balasore), Brahmani, and so on in Odisha. Similarly, he invokes the traditions of art, sculpture, temple architecture, costumes, as well as the journey of travellers who came to Odisha from Arabia and Persia. The poetry of Dinakrishna and that of Chaitanya Dev too comes handy to support Kar's claims.

At the end of this survey, largely based on myth, hearsay and speculations, Birupakhya Kar turns to the present with a sense of sadness. He reflects pensively: 'Today, the name of Odisha is not uttered in lands and nations that have excelled in maritime activities. The Odias seem fearful of the sea; they are socially ostracized when they travel abroad by sea. Afraid of swimming in the ocean, most Odias today amuse themselves by throwing coins into the sea and watch the antics of fishermen' (p. 280).

It would be seen that Birupakhya Kar's essay on the seafaring tradition of Odisha, while claiming to be 'historical' is based, for the most part, on legends, folklore, iconography, and poetry. He makes speculative claims and uses expressions such as 'It must have been so', 'Perhaps it was so', and so on. The attempt at producing historiography of the Western kind signals the yearning for rationality, objectivity, and empiricism—all parts of colonial modernity. Ultimately, this desire fails because of an inability to provide a recorded history. The claim to a glorious and golden past remains a recurrent feature. However, it is a past that is idealized, given the existing crisis of identity.

Anthropocentrism

The conflicting approach to writing history continues to be manifest in the pages of *Utkal Sahitya*. For instance, the same issue of the journal carries an essay called 'The Problem of World Religions', written as part of a serial by Kulamani Dash. The essay is a thinly veiled account of anthropocentrism. It attempts to prove that practically everything outside India can be traced back to Indian sources! This includes Indian religions, culture, and philosophy, and even geographical land masses. For instance, Dash claims that the 'Harayu' river of Persia is the 'Sarayu' of India (p. 122), the name 'Euphrates' is similarly drawn from the term 'Bharat'. The name 'Bharat' is turned into 'Pharat' and subsequently becomes 'Euphrates' in Persia. He surmises that 'Babylon', the capital city of Persia, on the bank of 'Pharat', is associated with 'Bhupalan', and possibly comes from 'Bhupal' (Bhopal) of India. Likewise, the 'Kousi' community that lives on the bank of the river 'Tigavu' of Persia arguably went from 'Kasi' or 'Varanasi' or 'Benares' in India. Quoting several European thinkers like Max Mueller and Sir William Jones, Kulamani Dash concludes triumphantly:

In our earlier essays we have tried to prove that belief in God and the Almighty went from the Vedas to Zenda Avasta, and subsequently to the Bible in a distorted and degraded form. Those who advocate the theory of evolution, what arguments can they show to counteract against this view? The proof and the evidence that we have furnished earlier, do they not defeat the claims of evolution? (p. 126)

Dash concludes his argument of the Vedas as the source of all religions in the following words:

We have travelled along the banks of the river of Dharma (Religion) and travelled to the source of the river. Koran and Bible have taken us to Zenda Avasta, and Zenda Avasta to the Vedas. We have not been able to travel further. Once there, we notice that the stream of Religion that flows from heaven is lost amidst a mound of ice. Are we therefore not correct in our belief that the Vedas are a source of all Religions?

While one can legitimately have respect for one's own religion and cultural traditions, Kulamani Dash clearly seems to have gone overboard in his sweeping claims and assertions. To believe in a comparative study of religions is one thing, but to argue that the world religions have only one source, namely the Vedas, and that the rivers and places in Persia are invariably named after Indian names is clearly farfetched. That this article was part of a series in *Utkal Sahitya* points to the fact that it seemed to enjoy editorial approval, unless the editor himself was trying to cater to different sides without endorsing any particular viewpoint or argument.

Modernity and the New Woman

The cry for female education was strongly echoed in *Utkal Sahitya* by many literary women in Odisha. Abanti Rao, the niece of the illustrious Madhusudan Rao, spells this out quite clearly in her address to a women's conference published in the journal. She writes (2005: 41–4):

The theme of this conference is the reform of women's education. Women will experience a feeling of incompleteness, a sense of non-fulfillment at home, in society and the nation, and proceed on a path of reform: this is the aim of this conference. But who gets a sense of incompleteness? Only one who has acquired knowledge in a subject can realize the incompleteness of her knowledge. The ignorant does not understand the limits of her knowledge. Therefore, it is clear that Knowledge alone propels us along the path of reform. We must first understand this truth. Needless to say, the greater the spread of knowledge among women in Orissa, the faster would be the pace of progress for the family, society and the country. This is the reason, why this education reform conference is laying so much emphasis on primary education for girls of this province. We will have to universalize primary education and ensure that as far as possible, primary education becomes useful in the later life of the girls, and they reap the full benefit of this education when they enter family life. Woman is the focal point of the family. The family grows around her. Everyone knows the plight of the family where there is no woman. Lives of many women demonstrate to what extent they can engender the welfare of the family, society and the nation when their innate goodness is refined by education and gets tested by life. God has made women and men complementary to each other. Though man works in the external environment and woman generally stays at home, their companionship strengthens one another in their respective spheres of work. In our country, therefore, woman is called the *sahadharmini* of man. The woman who is a genuine *sahadharmini* of her husband can be said to be on the right path. When I say *sahadharmini*, I mean full co-operation between the husband and the wife and their like-mindedness in all matters. Can this ideal ever be realized by a woman who remains steeped in ignorance? Though a woman is supposed to confine her activities mainly to home, though the household duties are her principal responsibility, it will not do if she chooses to remain content with this. If the social responsibilities are shouldered only by men, they are not likely to be discharged in a holistic manner. Society does not consist of men alone; women also form a part of it. Society should not be deprived of the innate qualities of women like love, forbearance, tender insight and spirit of service. How can the responsibilities of the society towards women be discharged unless women find a place and a role in it? One should not forget that behind the yeoman contribution of the great Rammohan and Vidyasagar to the cause of women, stand their mothers. Vidyasagar's mother lent her active support to social reform activities of her son. Though the influence of Rammohan's mother was not directly visible, the great reformer had inherited noble qualities from his mother by birth.

Now days, we are passing through a critical time. The problems of society are giving rise to unrest. Our society and country are increasingly coming under western influence. For various reasons, our old values are getting eroded. Women should extend their gracious hands to lead society along the path of peace and prosperity at a time like this. Their conscience and their sagacity should enable women to usher in a new society by reconciling the best in the old values and the new.[7]

If Abanti Rao wished the emancipation of women through reforms and social action, others like Sarala Devi and Kuntala Kumari[8] did so through their creative and critical work. Literary women in Odisha had their role models in Bengal who, in turn, were influenced by the developments in the West. Emphasis was on the need for gradual change and not through radical feminist politics. In this the Odia women were greatly influenced by their Bengali counterparts, although their creative work was based on their own understanding and was distinctly homegrown.[9] The modernity project for Odia women was distinctly different from the way it was envisaged by the colonial administration, as indicated in the Introduction.

Travel and Contact Zones

Utkal Sahitya seems to have had a penchant for travel and travelogues. Some of the pieces published dealt with visits within the country and inside Odisha. However, the more prominent travel pieces related to visits abroad, to England, Japan, and the Middle East. 'Mesopotamia Jatra' (Journey to Mesopotamia) is a good instance of this kind. The travel pieces were meant to educate and enlighten the readers by bringing the culture and lifestyle of people who were regarded as distinct from Indians.

Thanks to the colonial impact, the sense of insularity was ruptured; a large number of people travelled involuntarily as migrant workers to distant and faraway places like Fiji, the Caribbean islands and the Guianas. Many Odias left the Indian shores through the port of Calcutta as indentured labour, along with their counterparts from U.P.

and Bihar, and were never heard of again. Their stories and experience on board the leaking ships remain untold.

The travel accounts that find place in *Utkal Sahitya* belong to a different category. Written by relatively well-to-do middle-class individuals, they are primarily meant for fellow beings in Odisha who had the memory of a maritime culture, but had no direct contact with this tradition in the present times. Serially narrated, 'Journey to Mesopotamia'[10] is told with great passion and fascination by Ramakrishna Tripathy. As a clerk or possibly a functionary in the postal department, he shares his great joy with the readers:

When I set foot on the deck of the ship 'Franz Ferdinand' on 4.11.1919 and gazed at the slowly disappearing coast of Bombay, my heart was filled with a great sense of joy. The sense of displeasure that I associated with the Postal department was turned into happiness. I had the privilege of a unique experience that few had in their life time. I stood atop the ship, and it left the shore of Bombay for Mesopotamia as its destination. (p. 159)

Tripathy explains graphically the motion of the ship, the sound of the engine, and the way it is slowly piloted out of the harbour. Instead of Odisha, he now bids farewell to Bombay (read India). Instead of the lights of the port and the city's skyline, he now sees complete darkness all around him. It is only the colonial empire that makes possible such a trip. The experience is being shared with others back home. There is, of course, a sense of fear, mixed with a tinge of desire to meet the unknown.

The author's attention is drawn to a flying fish by a fellow passenger, apparently a Bengali gentleman. 'I went,' he says, 'and stood where others watched the flying fish,' while making the following observation:

I would throw my gaze at the spots where the fish was expected to be around; then would look at the sea, keenly watching the scene lest the fish would leap and fly away. Thinking so, I would survey the sky and then look down. If only the fish would come up, I would succeed in my mission. Unsuccessful I returned to my chosen place. (p. 161)

We are informed that the ship contained mostly government officials and coolies. They all spoke Hindustani, a language unknown to the author. The inability to converse leads to amusing and humorous results. *Bistar* which means 'bedding' in Hindi, is mistaken as 'house' by Tripathy. In the next instalment of the travelogue, the author tells us of the arrival of the ship in Mesopotamia. There is no fear of the unknown given the fact that the land was full of Indians. He savours local fruits and spots Arabs and Jews. He sees the land made up of only two classes: the rich and the poor. He observes the lifestyle of a cross section of society and comes to the conclusion that unlike Indians, the people here were not quarrelsome and led a contented life full of physical and mental happiness. Tripathy's travel is mediated by the empire.

Colonial Travel

Tripathy's journey to Mesopotamia is characterized entirely by the spirit of colonialism. He owes the travel to the dictates of the imperial bureaucracy. He travels in the ship assigned to him. He sees the Arabs and Jews, as well as fellow Indians, always in binary terms: rich and poor. He makes blanket statements and concludes that the people here were not 'quarrelsome'. Behind the façade of peace, he is unable to see that the land he visits is full of colonial servitors. Deeply implicated in the colonial system, he cannot come up with independent angles of vision and action. The 'freedom' he enjoys in the journey is misleading since it is basically a guided tour. He has neither the agency nor the resources to undertake voyages that are truly independent. Travel is at once a condition and consequence of colonial modernity.

Travel as Initiation Rites

If travel to Mesopotamia brings to the minds of the Odia readers tidings of the British empire, there is no less interest in and curiosity about the mother country, Britain. Several travel accounts in *Utkal Sahitya* depict the experience of the travel of Odias to England. Sailabala Das's letters to her countrymen from England describe in detail about the journey on board the ship, the food habits of the British, the civic and political life of Englishmen, the meeting with the queen at Buckingham Palace, and other aspects. She brings to the attention of her people back home the lessons she learns; she observes the behaviour of the British towards their servants in England vis-à-vis the ill-treatment of the natives by Englishmen in India.[11]

On board the ship, Sailabala had the opportunity to closely observe English men and women. This is how she describes her experience with great insight and humour:

I had been told that the English ate a lot more than we could. My fifteen days' experience on board the ship convinced me that this indeed was the case. At six in the morning the servants brought them tea, bread, butter, biscuits and some fruit. The English passengers did full justice to these. Then, at nine a.m., when the bell for breakfast went off, they would proceed to the dining hall. There, on the table would be laid out rice, and ten or twelve curries made from fruit, fish, meat, eggs, and vegetable. These were to be washed down with lemonade, ice and soda. The passengers helped themselves to whatever they liked. Around 10.30 a.m. some were served beef soup and biscuits. Those who did not fancy this, were served milk and biscuits. At one p.m. they went to the dining hall for lunch. For lunch, as for breakfast, there would be all kinds of dishes laid out on the table. Afternoon tea was served at four. The passengers could have bread, butter, semolina pudding and cakes with their tea or coffee. At seven in the evening they would again be served dishes made from fish or meat. For supper at nine thirty p.m., they had bread, butter and mutton sandwiches. Thus, they would keep eating all day whatever they fancied.

The English were highly favored by the goddess for appetite. Those who get to see the quantity of food the English consumed will find what I say incredible. Every ship stored food for its passengers which would last for two months. The store-room of the ship resembled a small city. This would be filled from floor to ceiling with vegetables like cabbages, cauliflowers, potatoes, onions, peas, brinjals, and spinach. Readers can well imagine the quantity of vegetables required for feeding 800/900 passengers daily for two months. Surprisingly these vegetables stayed fresh for such a long period. One room of the ship was stored with ice and this room lay adjacent to the one in which vegetables were kept. For this reason the vegetables did not rot and stayed fresh. Imagine how many cows would be needed to get milk for so many passengers! And how much space and how much fodder would be needed for a herd of cows on board for two months! But the clever and sharp-witted English had found a way around this difficulty. When the ship left the shores of English big cans filled with milk were kept buried in ice. Frozen milk stayed absolutely fresh for two months. Milk, which goes sour in two hours if it is not boiled, remains unspoilt for long two months, thanks to the ingenuity of the English.

In our country, we do not bother to change our clothes when we eat. But, for the English, this simply is not done. No matter where they find themselves—at home, abroad or on board—they must change into something before they have a meal. At 6.30 p.m. a bell went off and the English passengers would go to their room, have a change of clothes, comb their hair and come to the dining hall.[12] (Das 2005: 56–7)

Sailabala goes to England for higher studies at the beginning of the twentieth century. She returns to Odisha, takes charge of the Ravenshaw Girls' school at Cuttack and plays a pioneering role in the field of women's education and social reforms movement in Odisha and Bihar, as they were known then. Travel becomes a catalytic agent for individuals like Sailabala to bring in Western modernity to India through education. Unlike Tripathy, Sailabala offers resistance to colonialism: She chooses her team and her destination regardless of her father's or the commissioner of education's wish; she refuses to go to Buckingham Palace in a gown, and insists that she be allowed to go in her sari; she does not visualize the customs and habits of people on board the ship, or at London through the eyes of the British or Anglophiles, of whom there must have been plenty before, during and after the voyage. She is amused to see the gluttony of the British on board the ship and feels a mixture of dismay and sadness when she thinks of the hunger and famine of her own country, caused by the British rule. She refuses to be intimidated by the might of the empire, and comes back to Odisha with her spirit intact. If she is transformed by her travel, it is by becoming more intrepid as a woman and a spirited lover of her country.

Others like Annada Shankar Ray who began his life as a poet and writer in Odia and travelled to England as an aspirant for higher education and career in the Indian Civil Service (ICS), wrote 'Bilati Chhithi' (Letters from England) for the benefit of fellow Odias in *Utkal Sahitya*.[13]

Annada Shankar begins his letter by date marking it: 'On board the Kaiser-I-Hind Ship, Mediterranean Sea, 13.8.1927'. He informs the readers that on account of the sudden flood in the river Baitarani, he could not travel to Bombay via Calcutta, and instead had to journey from Cuttack through Vijayawada, Secunderabad, Wadi to Bombay. His language is conversational and colloquial and he establishes an immediate rapport with the audience. He notices the difference in costume, dress, and lifestyle between the Odias and the southerners. He observes the relative affluence of even ordinary passengers in the South vis-à-vis their Odia counterparts.

There are plenty of details that inform the readers of the development in the railways: the Bengal–Nagpur Railways (BNR) and the Indian Peninsular Railway (of the Nizam's estate) take him to Victoria Terminus in Bombay. He is impressed by the sights, spectacles, and cityscapes in the metropolis and tells us of Malabar Hill, the habitation of the rich. Impressed by the spectacles, he spots a large number of young women moving around freely in the city. There is no segregation of the sexes here. Like Sailabala, Annada Shankar cannot help thinking about the sad situation of women back home in Odisha. A staunch believer in women's rights (he was a mentor to the noted Odia literary feminist Sarala Devi), Annada Shankar writes:

The women of Bombay unlike our womenfolk do not remain confined to the Purdah. They do not wither like a creeper at the sight of a male. Suddenly I found them 'attacking' my hostel in the afternoon with books and notebooks in their hands. They were neither very old nor young; they did not suffer from a sense of embarrassment. I stepped out with a sense of trepidation and found groups of women, young, middle aged and old, moving around freely. They did not look odd in the company of men. While the question of rights for women appears odd in our society, in South India, it has become fairly commonplace. We would do well to follow their model. There would be greater spread of girls' education. There would be no problem of girls' conveyance to schools; nor the problem of lady teachers. Women would enjoy better health care and the cities would be free from child mortality and tuberculosis. (p. 223)

Westernization and Western modernity for Annada Shankar are certainly boons for securing the emancipation of Indian women. At the same time, he is not unmindful of the 'baneful' aspects of Western 'modernity'. He is aware that 'due to the fact that the Bombay city was modeled after the West, there was a conflict between the owners of industries and workers here'. He concedes that he has only heard of this and not seen it with his own eyes, given the relatively short time he stayed in the city. But the point is made.

Annada Shankar provides meticulous details of the ship 'Kaiser-I-Hind' and lists the international passengers it carried from Bombay, via Port Said. The elaborate living arrangements on board the ship, the drawer, dressing table, berths, the smoking room, the food, the saloon for listening to piano, the library, everything, he says, was done in the 'Bilati style'—it was indeed a microcosm of the England he would step into soon.

Imperial Gateways

In all this, Annada Shankar seems to pay insufficient attention to the role of the British empire and the way it was shaping the attitude of the aspiring middle-class elites in their iconic desire for education, position, and progress. The sites he passes through—the Red Sea, the Arabian Sea, the Suez Canal, Port Said, Egypt, Tripoli, and Algeria—all of them are no doubt sea passages, but they are also imperial gateways that facilitate the voyage to England. One still has to go through Gibraltar, Marseilles, Calais, and the English Channel to reach London. The voyage thus becomes part of the discovery of the West and the journey more than a passage; it is an initiation rite to a new world. Annada Shankar shares his fascination about the colonies of the British empire. He is less mindful of the suffering and subjugation of the colonized subject, the plight of his own people, and eventually chooses to be part of the colonial bureaucracy; he joins the ICS.

As in the case of Sailabala and Annada Shankar, others wrote about journeys to shores elsewhere and destinations that were valorized. 'Japan Jatra' of Kailashchandra Bharatkara in *Utkal Sahitya*[14] signals a desire to travel to an eastern nation that had acquired importance and prestige in the eyes of Indian writers and intellectuals.

Bharatkara's journey commences on 29 July 1906, two decades prior to that of Annada Shankar. The journey by sea for him is a constant source of fascination; there is no detail here that is trivial and commonplace and that can be left out. He regrets that due to a sudden change in plans, he could not meet his friends, barring two before he set sail. The first day was spent witnessing the exquisite greenery of the river Ganges on both sides and soon they found themselves in the Bay of Bengal. Details like sea sickness are explained for the benefit of people back home. A halt in the port city of Rangoon leads to a visit to the pagodas situated in a wide and clean city. While he has to remove his shoes, he cannot help notice that the 'Westerners could enter with shoes on' (p. 272).[15] He visits other spots such as the Royal Lake of Rangoon, the Saw Mill which used elephant labour, and spots men and women in traditional costume and appropriate headgear. Here too, as in Bombay, women enjoy freedom; everywhere one sees a larger presence of women who are distinctly 'cleverer than men' (p. 272).

From Rangoon, the voyage took Bharatkara to Penang in Malaysia. In Penang, which is occupied by the British, he sees the small island comprising hillocks, waterfalls, and coconut and rubber plantations. He visits the famous Chinese temple on top of a mountain and is impressed by the ancient texts, temple sculpture, and architecture. From Penang, he travels to Singapore, which again is under British occupation. Cane work is widely sold here. A train journey to Johor takes him to the palace of the sultan and to a licensed gambling house. Back in Singapore he visits the botanical garden and museum.

From Singapore he voyages to Hong Kong—again, a British colony. He is impressed to see warships and cable cars, the latter linking hillocks. He describes the costume, footwear, ornaments, and the dressing habits of the Chinese men and women and spots the boathouse where many live.

From Hong Kong the ship proceeds to Shanghai in China. In the turbulent China Sea, he spots many flying fish. At Shanghai, he visits the public garden maintained by foreigners. He is astonished to find the notice which forbids the entry of 'dogs and Chinamen' (p. 274). Three days later, he reaches the old port of Nagasaki.

Similarly, 'From Tokyo to Calcutta' by Mahesh Chandra Ray in the journal[16] gives a graphic account of the Japanese social, cultural, and political scene. Details are provided about the city of Tokyo in an elaborate manner. Parks, gardens, military museums, schools, colleges, and zoos are all brought in and create a sense of awe in the reader. The military prowess of the ordinary Japanese children and adolescents are contrasted with the so-called cowardice of their Russian and Chinese counterparts ('the teachers said that the Japanese may be short in height, but they are more courageous than the Russians') (p. 188). The fact that Japan excelled because of the Western impact and modernization seems to be the underlying refrain by the author (pp. 187–91).

What is remarkable about the accounts of Bharatkara, Mahesh Chandra and Annada Shankar is the elaborate manner in which travel by sea is described. The passage through British colonies and protectorates tell them and the reader about the vastness of the British empire and the position of natives under the British rule. Travel becomes a means of identity and self-definition under the colonial rule. The Indians, Malays, Chinese, and Singaporeans are seen as colonial subject, worthy of curiosity, but it is the British that are feared and respected. Colonialism is overpowering, and colonial travel, for the most part, seeks to further Western modernity.

Colonial Transactions

The influence of English literature[17] is seen in the many translations/adaptations that were published in the journal. For instance, *Utkal Sahitya*[18] published Shelley's 'To the Skylark' under '*Bharata Pakhyi Prati*' (pp. 104–6). Translated by Narayan Mohan De, the piece is a vivid rendering of the poem by Shelley. Similarly, we see the adaptation of a story by Maupassant, called '*Bhadra*', authored by Pratibha

Devi,[19] the daughter of the editor of *Utkal Sahitya*, Biswanath Kar (pp. 598–601). Other essays such as 'Ravi Varma's Art Treasures' tell us of the interest created in Odisha by an art exhibition at Cuttack's Haripur Ghat in 1996 held by the author Shashibhushan Ray (pp. 226–31).[20] Ray is conscious of the widespread reputation of Ravi Varma in many parts of India and is keen to bring him and his art to Odisha. As he observes: Thanks to English education, we have had the benefit of exposure to new developments in literature. Regrettably, the same impact is not seen with regard to Art. We have not had the good fortune to see English and European painters such as Raphael...[21]

He outlines the reasons responsible for this state of affairs. The major factor, he points out, is the difference between the Eastern and Western art form in terms of approach and style. He underlines the importance of an exposure to the best of Indian art that has been influenced by the West.

The impact of Western institutions on India may be seen in the essay 'The Founder of the Kindergarten System of Education: Mahatma Frobel' by Chandrasekhar Nanda (pp. 187–96), '*Karma Beera Booker T Washington*' by Jagabandhu Singh (pp. 11–22),[22] 'Roman Rolland and Tolstoy' (pp. 204–9)[23] by Pratibha Devi and 'The Evolution of English Poetry' by Pratip Sen (pp. 381–6).[24] The effort here, as else-where, is to try and acquaint the Odia readers with the best of English and Western literature and culture.

———

English education, the New Woman, scientific historiography, sea voyages, new cultural codes, widow remarriages, plagiarism, tax systems, photography and cosmetics—myriad such issues found expression in *Utkal Sahitya* during its lifetime. As we have seen, the editor and the contributors negotiated with the issues in varied terms and made the journal one of the finest mediums in Eastern India.

Biswanath Kar sought an affiliation to an earlier literary–critical tradition that had been lost and marginalized, thanks to the colonial

interventions. He tried to fashion out an indigenous imaginary, com-
bining the best of the colonial and alternative modernity.

Notes

1. Chandramohan Maharana was a close colleague of Biswanath Kar, a
well-known contributor.

2. Edited by Biswanath Kar, the inaugural issue dated 1897 was printed by
B.P. Das at the Arunodaya Press. The issue carried poems, essays on various
topics, literary criticism, addresses, songs of a large number of contributors,
many of whom were eminent in their own times. They include authors like
Madhusudan Rao, Shashibhushan Ray, Reba Ray, Fakir Mohan Senapati,
Sadhu Charan Ray, Nilamani Bidyaratna, Damodar Patnaik, Krushnaprasad
Choudhury, Chandramohan Maharana, Gangadhar Meher, Nandakishore Bal,
Sadashib Bidyabhushan, Rajnarayan Das, and others. The journal would main-
tain its standard for nearly half-a-century even after the death of its founder.

3. All translations from Odia into English used in the chapter, unless
otherwise indicated, are by me.

4. *Utkal Sahitya*, Issue 3700, No. 5, pp. 135–62. All page references,
henceforth, are parenthetically given in the text; details provided in the end-
notes.

5. There are a number of Odia travel texts before and following
Shashibhushan Ray. See, for instance, Basudev Sudhal Dev, *Chitrotpala*
(1893); Bhubanananda Das, *Bilatpatra* (1914); Damodar Patnaik, *Kapilasa
Jatra* (1885); Gobinda Rath, *Kalikata Bhramana* (1875), *Lat Darshan*
(1885); Shashibhushan Ray, *Utkal Prakruti* (1911). See also Manmath
Kumar Pradhan, 'Odiya Bhramana Sahitya: Eka Mukhashala', Balasore:
Subarnashree, IV (2, 2006).

6. *Utkal Sahitya*, Kartika, 1328 Sala, No. 7.

7. *Utkal Sahitya*, 33/11.6, Bhadra Ashwina, 1336 Sala. See also Devi
(1983), Devi (1934) and Haripriya Devi, 'Bandini Nari' (Woman the
Prisoner), *Utkal Sahitya*, November 1940. Many of the Odia literary women
like Kuntala Kumari find a place in *Early Women's Writings in Orissa, 1898–
1950* (2005). A number of them like Kokila Devi, Narmada Kar, Suprabha
Devi and Reba Ray made their debut in the pages of *Utkal Sahitya*.

8. For a good instance of creative works by Odia literary women that captures a blending of tradition and modernity, see Kokila Devi, 'Bilasini', *Utkal
Sahitya*, No. 20/5, 1915. See also Dash (1969).

9. For a good account of women's personal narratives in Bengal, see Karlekar (1971). For a perspective from early history of women's writings in America, see Kelly (1985).

10. *Utkal Sahitya*, Shrabana, 1327.

11. For Sailabala's writings and life, see her autobiography *A Look Before and After* (1956).

12. The article appeared serially in the following issues of *Utkal Sahitya*: No. 12/2, Jeystha, 1311 Sala, pp. 41–5; No. 12/3, 1315 Sala, pp. 71–81; No. 13/1, Baisakha, 1316 Sala, pp. 1–7. For a reading of the feminist texts in Odisha, see Mohanty (2008).

13. *Utkal Sahitya*, Issue 3100, No. 6.

14. *Utkal Sahitya*, Issue 1400, No. 11.

15. *Utkal Sahitya*, Issue 1400, No. 11.

16. *Utkal Sahitya*, Issue 1400, No. 11.

17. For an excellent study of the coming of English literature to India, see Viswanathan (1989).

18. *Utkal Sahitya*, Issue 1800, No. 2.

19. *Utkal Sahitya*, Issue 2900, No. 11.

20. *Utkal Sahitya*, Kartika, 1315.

21. Quoted in *Utkal Sahitya*, Kartika, 1315.

22. *Utkal Sahitya*, Issue 1500, No. 1.

23. *Utkal Sahitya*, Magha, Vol. 37, No. 11.

24. *Utkal Sahitya*, Magha, Vol. 37, No. 11.

Conclusion

> *And how are our subjects to be formed to disposition thus favorable*
> *to us, to be changed thus in their character, but by new principles,*
> *sentiments, and tastes, leading to new views, conduct and man-*
> *ners; all of which would, by one and the same effect, identify their*
> *cause with ours, and proportionately separate them from opposite*
> *interests?*
>
> —Charles Grant[1]

Charles Grant's panacea for the ills India suffered from would be
voiced in terms of Western literature and Christianity (Viswanathan
1998: 72). It is not by the display of brute power or the superior-
ity of one's system of polity and governance, he declared, that one
could ensure 'permanent and ... indissoluble'[2] ties with India, but
by 'the superior moral conduct of the Britons', based on a set of fine
'religious and moral principles'. The belief in a superior moral and
religious conduct of the ruling class and 'superior moral and religious
principles' inherent in the British race, are taken to be a self-evident

fact for Grant; his disparagement of the Indian systems of thought and moral universe is the evidence of his prescriptive order in the narrative of amelioration.

In a varying way, the world view of Grant and others would define the contours of the colonial modernity project in India. Western modernity came to Odisha, indeed to the whole of the subcontinent, as we have seen in this work, in a complex and many-sided manner. The European Enlightenment with its belief in the capitalized 'Virtues' of 'Rationality, Universality and Progress', impacted the educational, cultural, and political institutions of India through the British rule. Such modernity can well be defined as colonial in character. Essentially Janus-faced, it attempted to bring about reforms, wherever it could, without upsetting the traditional social order.

The year 1866 has been important as a point of departure for our study: It witnessed the great Odisha famine and led to the birth of *Utkal Dipika*, the first major news periodical of Odisha, a weekly founded and edited by Gourishankar Ray. Similarly, on 1 April 1936, a large part of the Odia-speaking areas was brought together by the British who had arrived earlier in the province in 1803. In between, in 1897, the eminent Odia reformist–litterateur Biswanath Kar founded *Utkal Sahitya*. Both *Utkal Dipika* and *Utkal Sahitya* ran beyond the lifespan of the two editors who left an outstanding legacy after them. The two journals were the best of their kind and were representative of the principal genres.

In terms of contents and style, the two were manifestly different; one was primarily a news weekly, the other a literary periodical. Both complemented each other, their lifespan coincided during the period between 1897 and 1927. Both were born essentially as cultural and political responses to the challenges Odisha faced in the mid nineteenth century for its survival. There seems to have been a sense of inevitability in the emergence of the two forums, given the political contexts of the times. However, by the first decades of the twentieth century, certainly by the 1920s, the basic objective of the two journals, namely the need to safeguard the language and literature of the region, was achieved. To be sure, further battles lay ahead. But in the social, political, and cultural arena, Odisha had gone beyond the crisis point; its survival was no longer in doubt.

Gourishankar and Biswanath were essentially the products of their times. They were nativists and modernists who were open to the ideas of change. Indeed, they saw change as inevitable. Through their writings and actions, many of which have been chronicled in this book, they used the breath of the new culture, winds of change blowing from within and outside the province, to act as the life force that would sustain an older civilization. Many of the changes that the West propelled, such as the new system of education, style of governance, use of technology and warfare, maritime trade, land, revenue, agricultural and irrigation system, costume, food and entertainment industry, (the shampoo bath and the polo game to mention at least two), and the progressive agenda in the different domains of life—all came as vast challenges to a traditional social order.

Challenges

The challenge that Gourishankar and Biswanath faced was to harness the strength of the Western modernity for the benefit of an insular province. While they admired some aspects of the European modernity, they would not endorse Grant's views and prescriptions for the salvation of Odisha. Indeed, they promoted a critique of colonial modernity in their pages through satires and lampoons. The best of Fakir Mohan's writings, especially his *Chha Mana Atha Guntha* and tales like 'Dakamunshi' and 'Patent Medicine', as we have seen earlier, are evidence to this fact.

The editors were not rationalists and secularists. Basically religious-minded and reformist in temperament, members of the Brahmo Samaj, the first of the two was a Kayastha by birth, and the second was born a Brahmin. While Gourishankar remained a staunch Kayastha throughout his life, and upheld the 'virtues' of his caste through the activities he spearheaded for its welfare, by contrast, Biswanath was an iconoclast Brahmin, regarded as renegade by his community. He discarded the emblems of his caste in favour of the larger affiliation to humanism. Both of them were outstanding individuals, organized, dedicated, idealistic, and intellectually gifted with a creative approach to life. They contributed to the making of an alternative modernity with marked shortcomings.

For instance, it must be said that the journals made insufficient effort in exposing the exploitation in the hinterland, especially in the feudatory kingdoms. While they received patronage from the feudal elements and the kings, they did not speak out enough against the feudal kingdoms and forces. Their complicity with the ruling class in Odisha and Britain would weaken their nationalist ardour and the desire to construct a full-fledged vernacular modernity. Regardless of the strategic choice they made for the sake of exigency, they stand ill accorded with an anti-colonial position. Clearly, the ideological fault lines would remain buried in the province, and would surface in the decades following the thirties of the last century.

Modernity Agenda

Dipika promoted the agenda of colonial modernity and its alternative at the same time. It brought in perspectives from far and near, ran excerpts from other magazines and journals published in India and abroad. In specific terms, it underlined the importance of debating clubs and public speeches in creating a new public culture in Odisha, handled by members of the elite. It used a mix of wit, humour, and solemnity to highlight important literary, cultural, and political issues. And finally, in a masterly manner, it dealt with the issue of language politics. The attempts to impose the Bengali language and script were brilliantly parodied in *Utkal Dipika*. It created the necessary public awareness about the linguistic, literary, and cultural pride among the Odias and made strategic alliances with individuals and forces for the preservation of the Odia language and culture.

In a varying manner, a similar trend may be found in *Utkal Sahitya* as well. The new cultural codes, menace of plagiarism, imperialism and war, modernity and new historiography (the latter exemplified by the diaries of the Portuguese trader Streynsham Master), rise of the New

Woman, travel and contact zones—all find a prominent place in the journal. Likewise, it played an outstanding role in debating issues like modernity and the reform agenda, the role of leadership, the question of self-reliance, and cultural transactions between the English and Odia. It employed a variety of literary styles and encouraged a wide range of genres, such as prose, poetry, fiction, short story, essays, criticism, travelogues, skits, humour, and occasionally, plays. The best of the writers, poets, and essayists of modern Odisha like Fakir Mohan Senapati, Madhusudan Rao, Kuntala Kumari Sabat, and others wrote in this forum. They gave respectability to the journal, and in turn, found an excellent platform for self-expression and creativity. The writings of colonial travel it published showed both colonial affiliation and post-colonial yearnings.

Periodical press in Odisha had a fractured relationship and multifaceted negotiations with colonial modernity. This modernity was not consensual; it had many contestatory discourses surrounding it. The contestation turns out to be the defining moment in the history of colonial Odisha, its finest hour.

Notes

1. 'Observations on the State of Society Among our Asiatic Subjects', Great Britain, Parliamentary Papers, 1831–2, General Appendix, p. 80.

2. Charles Grant, 'Observations', pp. 8–80.

Bibliography

Print sources: books and articles

Acharya, Poromesh, 'Development of Modern Language Text-Books and the Social Context in 19th Century Bengal,' *Economic and Political Weekly*, 21 (17, 1986): 745–51.

Acharya, Pritish, 'Nationalist Politics: Nature, Objective and Strategy (From Late 19th Century to Formation of UPCC),' in P.K. Mishra (ed.), *Culture, Tribal History and Freedom Movement* (New Delhi: Agami Kala Prakashan, 1989).

Acharya, Sudarsana, *Unabinsha Satakara Duiti Bismruta Sahityapatra: Utkala Madhup, Pradipa* (in Odia) (Rourkela: Pragati Utkala Sangha, 2009).

Behera, Krushna Charan and Debendra Kumar Dash (eds), *Fakir Mohan Granthabali* (in Odia) (Cuttack: Grantha Mandir, 2000).

Bolton, John, *My Times and I* (Bhubaneswar: Orissa Sahitya Akademi, 1985).

————, *Essays on Oriya Literature* (Jagatsinghpur: Prafulla Pathagar, 2003).

Bolts, William, *Considerations on India Affairs*, Part II, (London: 1772).

Botein, Stephen, Jack R. Censer, and Harriet Ritvo, 'The Periodical Press in Eighteenth Century English and French Society: A Cross-Cultural Approach,' *Comparative Studies in Society and History*, 23 (3, 1981): 464–90.

Breckenridge, Carol A., Dipesh Chakrabarty, Homi K. Bhabha, and Sheldon Pollock (eds), *Cosmopolitanism* (Durham: Duke University Press, 2002).

Chakrabarty, Dipesh, *Provincializing Europe: Postcolonial Thought and Historical Difference* (New Delhi: Oxford University Press, 2001).

Chakravarti, Sudeshna, Sanjukta Dasgupta, and Mary Mathew (eds), *Radical Rabindranath: Nation, Family and Gender in Tagore's Fiction and Films* (Hyderabad: Orient Blackswan, 2013).

Chandra, Sudhir, 'Regional Consciousness in 19th Century India: A Preliminary Note', *Economic and Political Weekly*, 17 (32, 1982): 1278–85.

Chatterjee, Partha, *Nationalist Thought and the Colonial World: A Derivative Discourse* (London: Zed Books, 1986).

Das, J.P., *Desha, Kala, Patra* (in Odia) (Bhubaneswar: Prachi Prakashan, 1992).

———, *Sundardas* (Bhubaneswar: Grassroots, 2004).

Das, M.P., 'History of Early Oriya Printing', *The Orissa Historical Research Journal (OHRJ)*, Golden Jubilee, 1 (1984).

Das, Nabakumar, S.M. Srichandan Singh, K.M. Mallik and Shobha Ray (eds), *Karmaveer Gourishankar Samaranika* (in Odia) (Cuttack: Gourishankar Smruti Sansad, 1988).

Das, Sailabala, *A Look Before and After* (Cuttack: self-published, 1956).

———, 'Bilat Prabas' [Journey to England], in Sachidananda Mohanty (ed.), *Early Women's Writings in Orissa, 1898–1950: A Lost Tradition* (New Delhi: SAGE Publication, 2005), pp. 56–7. Translated from Odia by Jatindra Kumar Nayak.

Dash, Debendra Kumar, *Utkal Sammilani 1903–36* (in Odia) (Rourkela: Pragati Utkal Sangha, 2005).

———, *Madhusudan Das: The Man and His Mission* (Rourkela: Pragati Utkal Sangha, 1998).

Dash, G.N., 'Jagannath and Oriya Nationalism', in A. Eshman, H. Kulke, and G.C. Tripathy (eds), *The Cult of Jagannath and the Regional Tradition in India* (New Delhi: Manohar, 1971).

Dash, Kailash Chandra, 'Odisha During the 19th Century', in Sricharan Mohanty (ed.), *Shatabdira Nayak: Gourishankar* (in Odia) (Rourkela: Pragati Utkal Sangha, 1997).

Dash, Kunjabihari (ed.), *Kuntala Kumari Sabat Granthamala* (in Odia), Vols. 1 and 2, (Cuttack: Cuttack Students' Store, 1969).

Devi, Bidyutprabha, 'Pratighat' [The Assault], *Bidyut Prabha Granthabali* (in Odia) (Cuttack: Friends' Publishers, 1983).

Devi, Sarala, *Narira Dabi* (in Odia) [The Rights of Women] (Cuttack: Hindustan Granthamala, 1934).

Dhall, Manjusri, *The British Rule: Missionary Activities in Orissa, 1822–1947* (New Delhi: Har Anand Publication, 1997).

Giri, Arabinda, *Utkala Darpana* (in Odia) (Rourkela: Pragati Utkal Sangha, 2007).

Houghton, Walter (ed.), *The Wellesley Index to Victorian Periodicals* (Toronto: University of Toronto Press; London: Routledge, 1966).

Kar, Bauribandhu, *Odia Sahityara Samalochanatmoka Itihas* (in Odia) [The History of Odia Literary Criticism] (Kitab Mahal, 1989; rpt. Cuttack: Friends' Publishers, 2013).

Kar, Biswanath, *Utkal Sahitya* (in Odia) (Cuttack, 1897; rpt. Cuttack: Sahityika, 1972).

Kar, Krushna Chandra, *Bagmi Biswanath* (in Odia) (Cuttack: Rashtra Bhasha Samabaya Prakashan, 1983).

Karlekar, Malavika, *Voices from the Inner World: Early Personal Narratives of Bengali Women* (New Delhi: Oxford University Press, 1971).

Kelly, Mary, *Private Women, Public Stage: Literary Domesticity in Nineteenth Century America* (New York: Oxford University Press, 1985).

Mallick, Basanta Kumar, *Paradigms of Dissent and Protest: Social Movements in Eastern India* (New Delhi: Manohar, 2004).

Mansingh, Mayadhar, *History of Oriya Literature* (New Delhi: Sahitya Akademi, 1962).

Menon, Dilip, 'Religion and Colonial Modernity: Rethinking Belief and Identity', *Economic and Political Weekly*, 38 (17, 2002): 1662–7.

Mill, James, 'Periodical Literature', *Westminster Review*, 1 (1824): 206–49. Written anonymously by the author.

Mishra, Gopal Chandra, *Odishara Bikashare Patra Patrikara Prabhava* (in Odia) [The Impact of Odia Periodicals on the Development of Odisha] (Cuttack: Jashodhara Mishra, distributed by Grantha Mandir, 1979; rpt. 1983).

Mohanty, Banshidhar (ed.), *Atharasha Chhasathi* (in Odia) [Eighteen Sixty Six] (Cuttack: Friends' Publishers, 1978).

Mohanty, Bidyut, 'Orissa Famine of 1866: Demographic and Economic Consequences', *Economic and Political Weekly*, 28 (1 and 2, 1993): 55–66.

Mohan, Fakir, *Six Acres and a Third* (*Chha Mana Atha Guntha* [in Odia]), translated by Rabi Shankar Mishra, Satya P. Mohanty, Jatindra K. Nayak, and Paul St-Pierre (New Delhi: Penguin Books, 2006). First published by the University of California Press in 2005.

Mohanty, Kahnucharan, *Ha Anna* (in Odia), 10th Edition, (Cuttack: Sathi Prakashan, 1997). First published in 1934–5.
Mohanty, Nivedita, *Oriya Nationalism: Quest for a United Orissa in the 19th Century* (New Delhi: Manohar, 1982).
Mohanty, Panchanan, 'British Language Policy in 19th Century India and Oriya Language Movement', *Language Policy* (Netherlands: KP, 2002).
Mohanty, Pramod Kumar, *Colonialism and South Asia: Cuttack, 1803–1947* (Kolkata: R.N. Bhattacharya, 2007).
Mohanty, Sachidananda (ed.), *Early Women's Writings in Orissa 1898–1950: A Lost Tradition* (New Delhi: SAGE Publication, 2005).
———, 'Travel, Railroad and the Southern Imaginary: An Early Travel Narrative in Eastern India', *Gender and Cultural Identity in Colonial Orissa* (Hyderabad: Orient Longman, 2008).
———, *Literature and Social Reforms in Colonial Orissa: The Legacy of Sailabala Das* (New Delhi: Sahitya Akademi, 2006).
———, 'The Virtuous Woman in the Ideal Home: Female Identity and the Conduct Book Tradition in Orissa', in C. Vijayasree (ed.), *Writing the West: Representations from Indian Languages* (New Delhi: Sahitya Akademi, 2004).
———, 'Language Dialectic and Fakir Mohan's Rhetoric of Progress', in Ramanan, Mohan and P. Sailaja (eds), *English and the Indian Short Story* (Hyderabad: Orient Longman, 2000).
———, 'Rebati's Sisters: Search for Identity through Education', *India International Centre Quarterly*, 21 (4, 1994).
———, 'Autobiography as History: The Case of Fakir Mohan', *The Literary Criterion*, 31 (1 and 2, 1996).
——— (ed.), *Bismruta Prampara: Odia Sahiyatere Nari Pratibha: 1898–1950* (in Odia) (Kolkata: Sahitya Akademi, 2002).
———, 'Jayanta Mahapatra in Conversation with Sachidananda Mohanty', *South Asian Review*, 34 (2, 2013): 111–22.
Mohanty, Satya P. and Harish Trivedi, 'The Literary Review from Below: Fakir Mohan Senapati and Colonial Indian Society', *Economic and Political Weekly* 41 (46, 2006).
Mohanty, Satya P. (ed.), *Colonialism, Modernity, Literature: A View from India* (London: Palgrave Macmillan, 2009).
Mohanty, Sricharan, 'The Autobiography of Ananta Das' (in Odia), *Esana*, 57 (2008): 28–60.

Mohapatra, Bishnu, 'Ways of Belonging: The Kanchi Kaveri Legend and the Construction of Oriya Identity', *Studies in History*, 12 (2, 1996): 203–21.

Mrutyunjaya Granthabali (in Odia), Pratham Khanda, (Cuttack 1971).

Nanda, Phanindra Bhushan, *Sambalpur Hitaisini: Eka Adhyyana* (in Odia) (Bhubaneswar: Apurba, 2002).

———, *Sachidananda Tribhuban Dev* (in Odia) (Bhubaneswar: Orissa Sahitya Akademi, 2008).

Nandy, Ashis, *The Intimate Enemy: Loss and Recovery of Self under Colonialism* (Delhi: Oxford University Press, 1983).

Nayak, Ganeswar, 'The Orissa Famine of 1866', *The Newsletter of the Department of History*, Utkal University, 52 (winter 2009).

———, 'The Coastal Canal of Orissa during the Colonial Era', *Orissa Review*, (May–June 2010): 66–9.

Nayak, Jatindra K., *A World Elsewhere: Images of Kolkata in Oriya Autobiographies* (Bhubaneswar: Grassroots, 2010).

Nepal, Bhagirathi, *Bagmi Biswanath Kar* (in Odia) (Cuttack: K.K. Mishra & Co., 1984).

Patnaik, Gorachand, *The Famine and Some Aspects of the British Economic Policy in Orissa, 1866–1905* (Cuttack: Vidyapuri, 1980).

Pattanayak, Sudhakar, *Sambadapatraru Odisara Katha* (in Odia) (Cuttack: Grantha Mandir, 1972; rpt. 2011).

Patra, Kishore Mohan, *Orissa under the East India Company* (Delhi: Munshiram Manoharlal, 1971).

Pradhan, Atul Chandra, 'Press and Journalism in the Nineteenth Century Orissa', *Bharati–Utkal University Journal–Humanities*, 7 (13, 1973): 31–40.

———, 'Educational Uplift of Women in the Nineteenth Century Orissa', *Our Documentary Heritage*, Vol. 1, (Bhubaneswar: Orissa State Archives, 1988).

———, 'Cultural Awakening in Orissa, 1866–1903', *Utkal Historical Research Journal*, (6, 1995): 64–83.

Pykett, Lyn, 'Reading the Periodical Press: Text and Context', *Victorian Periodicals Review*, 22 (3, 1989): 100–08.

Rao, Abanti, 'Abhibhashana' [To the Women of Orissa], in Sachidananda Mohanty (ed.), *Early Women's Writings in Orissa, 1898–1950: A Lost Tradition* (New Delhi: SAGE Publication, 2005), pp. 41–4. Translated from Odia by Aurobindo Behera.

Rath, Pandit Mrutyunjay, *Karmajogi Gourishankar* (in Odia) (Cuttack: Navodaya Prakashan, 1997).

Rath, Radhanath, 'Karmavir Gourishankar Ray', in Nabakumar Das, S.M. Srichandan Singh, K.M. Mallick, Shobha Ray et al. (eds), *Karmavir Gourishankar Smaranika* (Cuttack: Gourishankar Smruti Sadan, 1989).

Ray, Alok, *Nineteenth Century Studies* (Kolkata: Bibliographic Research Centre, 1975).

Ray, Gourango Charan, 'Gourishankar: A Patriotic Journalist of Modern Nationalism', in Nabakumar Das, S.M. Srichandan Singh, K.M. Mallick, Shobha Ray et al. (eds), *Karmavir Gourishankar Smaranika* (Cuttack: Gourishankar Smruti Sadan, 1989).

Ray, Shashibhushan, *Dakhinatya Bhramana* (in Odia) (Cuttack: Cuttack Trading Company, 1896; rpt. 1921).

Samantaray, Natabar, *Odia Sahityara Itihasa: 1803–1920* (in Odia) [History of Oriya Literature] (Bhubaneswar: Grantha Mandir, 1964).

Shattock, Joanne and Michel Wolff (eds), *The Victorian Periodical Press: Samplings and Soundings* (Leicester: Leicester University Press; Toronto: University of Toronto Press, 1982).

Singh, Jagabandhu, *Grihalaxmi* (in Odia), Part 1, 1st edition, (Cuttack: Cuttack Trading Company, 1946).

Singh, S.M. Srichandan et al. (eds), *Smaranika: 75th Gourishankar Smruti Samaroha* (in Odia) (Cuttack: Gourishankar Smruti Sadan, 1999).

Sutton, Amos, *Orissa and its Evangelization* (Calcutta: Derly Wilkins and Sons, 1850).

The Stories of Fakir Mohan Senapati (Cuttack: Prachi Prakashan, 1991).

Tod, James, *Annals and Antiquities of Rajasthan or the Central and Western Rajput States of India*, Vol. 2, (London: Smith, Elder & Co., 1832).

Toynbee, G., *A Sketch of the History of Orissa: From 1803 to 1828* (Jagatsinghpur: Prafulla, 2005).

Viswanathan, Gauri, *Masks of Conquest: Literary Study and British Rule in India* (Delhi: Oxford University Press, 1998).

Walsh, Judith, 'The Virtuous Woman and the Well-Ordered Home: The Reconceptualization of Bengali Women and their Worlds', in Rajat Kumar Ray (ed.), *Mind, Body and Society: Life and Mentality in Colonial Bengal* (Delhi: Oxford University Press, 1995).

Wolff, Michael, 'Charting the Golden Stream: Thoughts on a Directory of Victorian Periodicals', *Victorian Periodical Newsletter*, 4 (3, 1971): 23–38.

Zimmerman, Enid, 'Art Education for Women in England from 1890–1910 as Reflected in the Victorian Periodical Press and Current Feminist Histories of Art Education', *Studies in Art Education: A Journal of Issues and Research*, 32 (2, 1991): 105–16.

Websites

http:/www.agratoday.in/news/index
http:/www.bl.uk/reshelp/findhelprestype/news
www.oxfordbibliographies.com/view/document
www.victorianweb.org

Index

About the Author

Sachidananda Mohanty was formerly Professor and Head, Department of English, University of Hyderabad. Currently, he is Vice Chancellor, Central University of Orissa, Koraput. He is the recipient of numerous national and international recognitions, including the Katha Award and fellowships from the British Council, the Fulbright Foundation, and the Salzburg Seminar. A contributing editor to the literary e-journal *Muse India* (www.museindia.com), he has published extensively in the fields of British, postcolonial, gender, and translation studies at the national and international levels. He has done pioneering work in the fields of archival research and cultural history of nineteenth-century India.